Thoughts on Leadership from a Higher Level

Thoughts on Leadership from a Higher Level

Leadership Lessons from the Bible

R. J. Stepansky

iUniverse, Inc.
Bloomington

Thoughts on Leadership from a Higher Level
Leadership Lessons from the Bible

Copyright © 2011 by R. J. Stepansky

All rights reserved. No part of this book may be used or reproduced by any means, graphic, electronic, or mechanical, including photocopying, recording, taping or by any information storage retrieval system without the written permission of the publisher except in the case of brief quotations embodied in critical articles and reviews.

iUniverse books may be ordered through booksellers or by contacting:

iUniverse
1663 Liberty Drive
Bloomington, IN 47403
www.iuniverse.com
1-800-Authors (1-800-288-4677)

Because of the dynamic nature of the Internet, any web addresses or links contained in this book may have changed since publication and may no longer be valid. The views expressed in this work are solely those of the author and do not necessarily reflect the views of the publisher, and the publisher hereby disclaims any responsibility for them.

Any people depicted in stock imagery provided by Thinkstock are models, and such images are being used for illustrative purposes only.

Certain stock imagery © Thinkstock.

ISBN: 978-1-4620-6728-2 (sc)
ISBN: 978-1-4620-6730-5 (hc)
ISBN: 978-1-4620-6729-9 (e)

Printed in the United States of America

iUniverse rev. date: 12/05/2011

Contents

Introduction: The Holy Grail of Leadership Knowledge 1
    The Bible's lessons are relevant today 2
    Your thoughts are important 7
    Interpret and apply the scriptures 8

Part 1 - General Leadership Guidance 11
    Trust that God loves us 11
    Align with God's plan 12
    Balance and harmony in the world 12
    God provides help 13
    Treat people with respect 14
    We are of one spirit and purpose 16
    Learn and grow 18
    Training must be practiced 19
    We have gifts to share 22
    Our journey and trials in life 23

Part 2 – Take the Bible's lessons to work 27
    Introduction 27

Leadership Topics 27
    Management by walking around 27
    Be proactive 30
    Learn from the master planner 32
    Know your sheep 34
    Reduce stress 37
    Communicate effectively 39
    Seek experienced guidance 40
    Leaders must delegate to succeed 42
    Team members have responsibilities 43
    Leaders have responsibilities to society 45

Vision and Strategy Development 49
Build your vision for the future 49
Elements of a strong vision statement 50
Create business plan strategies 53
Communicate the business plan 54
Get customers and stakeholders involved 58
Help people accept change 59
Break down communication barriers 62
Promote teamwork 64
Sell the strategy to all levels 65
The business we are not in 66
Develop performance parameters 67
Set aggressive goals 68

Customer and Market Focus 69
Nothing is new in the world 69
Respect your stakeholders 69
Be direct and honest with customers 70
Put yourself in their shoes 71
Deepen your customer understanding 73
Profits enable good works 74
Generate new life 75
Be persistent 76
Delegate responsibility 78

Knowledge Management 80
Measure and analyze performance 80
Develop a business review calendar 82
Data reporting is expensive 83
Real time data is best 84
Design effective information systems 84
Ensure performance data is reliable 85
Collect data frugally 86
Minimize historical data storage 88
Bring information to life 89
Train associates to use data effectively 89
Create positive feedback 90
Information should correct not criticize 91
Share best practices 92

Managing the Internal Process.................................95
    Maintain Christian values..............................95
    Take corrective action.................................96
    Minimize process variation.............................97
    Promote continuous improvement.........................99
    Create opportunities for customers....................100

Organizational Results..102
    Do not micromanage....................................102
    Reports must create action............................103
    Monitor competitors...................................104
    Develop partnerships..................................105
    Prepare for a crisis..................................106
    Stay focused on God...................................107

Human Resource Development......................................110
    Develop a common business language....................110
    Use words that evoke pictures.........................111
    Share business information............................113
    Recruit the best people...............................115
    Training reduces stress...............................116
    Recognize and reward associate skills.................118
    Plan for your replacement.............................118
    Review succession plans annually......................120
    Build a diverse organization..........................120
    Train people to interview job candidates..............121
    Drive out the fear of failure.........................123
    Use equitable performance reviews.....................123
    Communicate expectations to employees.................125
    Discipline to improve performance.....................127

Ethical Behavior..130
    Honesty is the foundation to build on.................130
    Avoid improprieties...................................130
    Maintain integrity to build trust.....................131
    Have a code of conduct................................132
    Communicate and enforce ethical standards.............133

Charity 134
    Charity is a priority. 134
    God helps people who help others 135
    Extend help to the disadvantaged 136
    Charity aligns us with God's plan 137
    Our goal at retirement. 139

Conclusion 141

Introduction
The Holy Grail of Leadership Knowledge

My journey to become a leader began with a desire to learn and a Christian faith as a moral foundation. College experiences reinforced these gifts and they led to a career as a leader in industry. The quest for the Holy Grail of leadership knowledge began with an across the border assignment that put my career on a new path.

My twenty-eight year career in leadership positions started with an assignment as a factory manager in Canada. It progressed to working with business leaders and managers around the world. I have many fond memories of working with leaders in Europe, Asia, and Australia, building and staffing factories in Russia and Mexico and integrating business acquisitions into the parent company. My first assignment is still my fondest memory. The Canadian Company gave me a well-furnished impressive office, which was much larger than my office in Chicago. Three experienced department managers and an administrative assistant reported directly to me and my boss was the President of the Canadian Company. Being in charge of people and reporting to a company president was a new experience for me. It made me feel a little uncomfortable since I had limited leadership experience. My thinking soon focused on what a leader should be doing in this situation.

One Sunday a section in the church bulletin titled, "Taking the scriptures home," inspired me. The question that came to mind was could the scriptures also have a place in business? This started me on a journey to learn more about the relationship between the Bible and business leadership practices. Leaders must address many topics to be successful with their work. This has been true throughout history.

Leaders and managers have studied, developed, and taught their skills all over the world for thousands of years. These instructors and practitioners had their own techniques and styles. For students, success or failure to become leaders depended on their ability to understand and apply what they learned. In modern times, educators have recorded these management practices in instructional books and delivered them at seminars ad infinitum. I have attended numerous seminars and read countless books. Many times two experts use different words to describe the same methods. Consultants build businesses around catchy phrases like *Lean Manufacturing, Performance Drivers, No Boundaries,* and *Peak Performance.* They seem to start with the same root stock concepts and theories, but for one expert the final bloom looks, like a rose, and for another it looks like a daisy. Ice cream vendors entice us with the, "flavor of the month," and it seems that management consultants try to sell the leadership practice of the month.

I often wondered if there was a common thread that forms the bases, the rootstock, from which the numerous theories and practices of modern leadership and management sprouted. Finding this *Holy Grail* of knowledge would make life easier. There would be a single source from which to draw knowledge and direct my actions. This would be much better than trying to sort through the numerous programs that consultants and authors sell. Instead of dissecting the blooms of the experts to see what was at the root, the roots of knowledge would be available for guidance to create my own blooms.

The *Holy Grail* of knowledge was closer at hand than I thought.

The Bible's lessons are relevant today

Sunday after Sunday during my career, I listened to the lessons of the Old and New Testaments read at services. It was obvious over time that there were many links between today's successful management practices used by executives all over the world and the lessons taught in the Bible. In hindsight, this should not have been a surprise. The word bible comes from the Greek word for books. The authors of these books were great prophets inspired and gifted by God with great knowledge and wisdom. Hebrews tells us God spoke through the prophets.

<u>Hebrews 1:1</u>
God, who at sundry times and in various manners spoke in time past unto the fathers by the prophets,

The prophets gave us books of wisdom. We hear affirmation of the respect people have for the Bible's value when they say "this cook book is the bible for cooks" or "this repair manual is the bible for mechanics." They affirm the wide spread belief that the Holy Bible is an authoritative work and a resource to answer questions and solve problems.

Can the ancient writings in the Bible still be relevant today as a source of knowledge and guidance in the high tech world of 24/7 news broadcasts, twitters, emails, computers, internet search engines, and cell phones? The answer is yes! The lessons of the past are relevant today. Most modern communications methods are just a means to flood us with information. They do not give the direction or the time proven knowledge that the Bible does to guide our personal and business conduct. The flood of information and communications can be detrimental if it clogs our minds with information that adds little value to our life. We need to keep clear minds that can focus on where we are going in life and use the best practices that the Bible offers to help us get there. In Romans, we hear that the scriptures are an important resource.

<u>Romans 15:4</u>
For whatsoever things were written aforetime were written for our learning, that we through patience and comfort of the scriptures might have hope.

This book will share with the reader how the Bible's lessons teach good business and leadership practices. The scripture it contains gives guidance for the management practices discussed. The Bible's revelations come from the knowledge acquired by the early prophets over hundreds of years of human development and by revelations from God through the prophets and His Son, Jesus Christ. I hope that this book helps to encourage the *WWJD* (What Would Jesus Do) campaign. Young people wore wristbands inscribed with the initials *WWJD* to remind them to pause and think about Jesus' teachings before they made an important decision. The Bible is a great resource to help make decisions. The world would be a better place if we all wore similar wristbands and stopped to think and consult the Bible before we acted.

The sum total of all the knowledge accumulated through the ages helps define the basic principles that guide successful managers today and throughout history. Good management practices are not of modern design. They have evolved and have been refined with the application of biblical lessons over time. Each new generation interpreted these lessons to guide them through the challenges that society faced with new norms and technologies. These evolved management practices are not restricted to the business world. We can apply these practices to improve family life and community welfare. Families, like businesses, need leadership and management to ensure they prosper. Matthew warns that the guidance we give by our actions and lessons to the next generation must align with God's commandments for us to gain His reward.

Matthew 5:19
Whosoever therefore shall break one of these least commandments, and shall teach men so, he shall be called the least in the kingdom of heaven: but whosoever shall do and teach them, the same shall be called great in the kingdom of heaven.

It is important to understand how the definition of leadership differs from that of management. They are distinctly different concepts. The leader has an inspirational role to create a vision for the future, form overall strategies, and be the gatekeeper for business values. Managers have duties that are more functional. They flesh out business strategies, communicate information, organize resources, set objectives, and goals, monitor results, and provide feedback. Some leaders find it difficult to manage. Managers must do detail work and for some leaders this saps their energy and patience. Detail work bogs down their ability to work and plan for the future, which is their first priority. The manager makes sure the train runs on time, but the leader ponders what the train business will be like in the future and how to prepare for it.

Leaders have special talents that allow them to make the transition from a management to a leadership position. Good managers may not be good leaders. They may not have the gift to be able to see into the future and create new visions for where the business should be in three, five, or even ten years. People have different gifts and one set of gifts is as good as the other. They are just different and we need them all for the business world to exist. The duties of a leader and manager are different, but they are both part of the same team and God is the head of that team. John tells us that God is the center of our world and we are each a unique branch but part of the same vine.

John 15:5
I am the vine, ye are the branches: He that abideth in me, and I in him, the same bringeth forth much fruit: for without me ye can do nothing.

My intention with this book is to provoke the readers to see how the Bible can guide them in their business career. The reader may agree or disagree with the content and application of scripture. Both outcomes are respected and profitable since they lead to further thought and understanding within us. A book should be a living document that reflects not only the author's concepts and ideas but also the thoughts and ideas of the reader provoked by the book's content. Do not consider this book a novel but rather a collection of thoughts presented in an organized fashion. Read the entire work or jump around and read the sections shown in the contents that interest you. I do not discuss the topics in great depth. Rather, I present broad stroke thoughts on important items in the business landscape. Entire books on the various topics are available and the reader is encouraged to pursue those topics that interest them in more depth. The interpretation and success in applying leadership lessons is always dependent on each individual's skill level.

Part 1 of the book is devoted to general leadership guidance and gives an oversight of what leaders do and how they perform their work guided by God's overall plan. Scripture passages from the King James Version of the Bible support the guidance. Reflect on them to see how you can apply the words written thousands of years ago in today's world. In many cases, the scriptures serve as reminders to us of the principles we should use to address a leadership topic. The scriptures do not talk directly about computer systems, emails, or video seminars. I have tried throughout the book to interpret and to apply this ancient guidance to a modern day world. This is not an easy task. The parts of the scriptures written as parables will take more time to reflect on and to apply. This is not an easy challenge. God gave the disciples the ability to understand and apply the parables. Luke tells us we must also strive to understand them. We can then apply them to enhance our modern day leadership skills.

Luke 8:10
And he said, Unto you it is given to know the mysteries of the kingdom of God: but to others in parables; that seeing they might not see, and hearing they might not understand.

In Part 2, I discuss specific leadership topics and the guidance available from the Bible to achieve success. These sections also discuss the application of the leadership topics to daily life in the home and community. It is up to us to practice the lessons taught in the scriptures. Mary instructed the waiters at the wedding feast at Cana to bring water for her Son that He then turned into wine. The simple but powerful instructions she gave the waiters are the same we should also apply to God's word in the Bible, that is to read and act on God's words.

John 2:5
His mother saith unto the servants, Whatsoever he saith unto you, do it.

Your thoughts are important
The journey through this book will be a richer experience if you add your own thoughts and comments. It will have greater value when it contains your annotations. These notes will be especially advantageous to people who meet in groups to share ideas to enrich the experience with a new book. Personal comments add to the fuel of heated discussion, debate and shared knowledge that moves us forward and makes us better.

Apply the insights gained in the book to your personal life as well as your business life. To be successful in business, it helps to practice the principles of good management in the home with the family. Practice makes perfect, and it will instill sound principles of conduct in each family member. Guidance given at home on how to interact with people and handle daily affairs is very critical. Many schools do not teach these topics. Each of us needs guidance and this need has been around for a long time. Deuteronomy tells us to share God's words and wisdom with children and all family members.

Deuteronomy 6:6-7
And these words, which I command thee this day, shall be in thane heart: And thou shalt teach them diligently unto thy children, and shalt talk of them when thou sittest in thine house, and when thou walkest by the way, and when thou liest down, and when thou risest up.

People have used experienced guidance throughout the ages to guide their actions through ever changing social norms. In ancient time, before books and electronic media, knowledge and history passed verbally from generation to generation in the form of stories. The family elders were the storytellers, and they were the honored repositories of ancient history and practices. We can only imagine the thrill the elder storytellers gave young people as they sat around evening fires to listen to these colorful stories and history lessons.

These stories gave a foundation from which the norms of society were established and carried from generation to generation. Each generation added new learning to the stories, and the lessons improved the lives of each succeeding generation. The scriptures carried on this tradition by giving us a written record of lessons we can live by. This inspired guidance helps us to address the many issues that arise at work and at home.

Jesus made it clear to us that we must build a solid foundation to create personal satisfaction. We need to listen and act upon His words in the Bible. Matthew reports Jesus' words:

<u>**Matthew 7:24-27**</u>
Therefore, whosoever heareth these sayings of mine, and doeth them, I will liken him unto a wise man, which built his house upon a rock: And the rain descended, and the floods came, and the winds blew, and beat upon that house; and it fell not: for it was founded upon a rock. And every one that heareth these sayings of mine, and doeth them not, shall be likened unto a foolish man, which built his house upon the sand: And the rain descended, and the floods came, and the winds blew, and beat upon that house; and it fell: and great was the fall of it.

Interpret and apply the scriptures

The Bible is the greatest story ever told. As with all historical records, it is subject to interpretation, which is dependent on the current norms in society. What was the author really thinking when the words were put down on paper? We need to ask this question of historical lessons when we try to apply them to today's world.

We need to interpret the scripture passages like a work of art. First step back and look at the whole picture. Then delve into the detail. Biblical interpretations change over time as new information is learned. The creation of new knowledge never stops because the universe constantly evolves new practices and life styles. The strength of the Bible is that its teachings are timeless and of such a fundamental quality that they will survive the ages.

The danger with new interpretations is that the original story can be lost in a fog of poor or self-serving ideas. We can lose direction if we lose touch with the original Biblical story. Misguided use of the Bible to control people's lives for personal gain has occurred often throughout history. Consequently, we have to understand that the foundations of the Bible are peace, love, and truth. We should avoid people who might try to lead us astray from these focal points. It takes work to seek knowledge from the Bible and apply it at work and at home. Psalms invites us to use God's words to help us as we seek knowledge now and in the future.

Psalms 90:17
And let the beauty of the Lord our God be upon us: and establish thou the work of our hands upon us; yea, the work of our hands establish thou it.

Part 1 - General Leadership Guidance

Trust that God loves us

We can become good leaders and managers by using the lessons in the Bible. We must first accept some simple facts to achieve this. Without this acceptance, we cannot expect to improve ourselves. First, we have to accept that God loves us unconditionally, and He gave us the lessons in the Bible to help us. For most people this is not a challenge, but many people struggle to understand God's role in their lives. Secondly, we need to accept that God created the universe with a plan in mind and that everything He created was for a reason, and He created nothing by chance. Human nature often makes us curious why things are the way they are. Scientists spend lifetimes to analyze creation and often fail to understand what creation really means. We may not fully understand the reasons behind many of God's creations, but we have to accept that there was a definite reason, a purpose for them. We are comforted to know that God is an all-generous and loving God. His creations are for our benefit. John's gospel tells us that God made all things.

> **John 1:1-3**
> In the beginning was the Word, and the Word was with God, and the Word was God. The same was in the beginning with God. All things were made by him; and without him was not anything made that was made.

Align with God's plan

Once we affirm a strong foundation in the belief of God, we can look at the link between Him and ourselves. Successful leadership at home or at work does not only come from the application of theory and practices. The path and work we choose must be in alignment with God's plans for the universe and the treatment He expects for His peoples across the globe. Throughout history, tyrants and dictators like Hitler have been deposed not because they had bad leadership skills or bad managers who worked for them. They lost their leadership position and power because their path and practices did not align with God's will. Moreover, the Bible teaches that God's plan for the world stresses peace and tranquility versus stress and mayhem. God expects leaders, who He gave the gifts of both ability and success, to deliver with His help, a good life to the people in their care. Consequently, greed and the sole pursuit of personal fame and money as drivers in business life will never be enough to satisfy us. These drivers alone will cause us to fall short of the potential we have and not reap true long-term satisfaction that work can give us when we help others. God makes His determination clear in Psalms to create peace and tranquility and eliminate mayhem and suffering. He wants us to work with Him to achieve this and travel together down the same path.

> **Psalms 46:9**
> He maketh wars to cease unto the end of the earth; he breaketh the bow, and cutteth the spear in sunder; he burneth the chariot in the fire.

Balance and harmony in the world

God created the world with balance and harmony at its core and science tells us how this works. One of the lessons I learned as a university engineering student is that simple rules and laws of balance explain most of the phenomena in nature. A typical example is the concept of mass-energy equivalence. It is a principle that states that the total energy of an object is constant. It either is in the form of radiant energy, like sunlight, or as energy stored in matter like coal. The famous equation, which governs this principle, is:

$$\text{Energy} = \text{Mass} * C^2 \text{ (C is a conversion constant)}$$

This equation says mass can be converted into energy. It allows a scientist to calculate the amount of energy the mass can generate. A good example is the burning of a piece of wood in a bonfire. We watch as the wood's mass diminishes while the energy released warms us. This principle shows a simple harmony and balance that exists in nature between matter and energy. The Bible reinforces this theory by stating that God's energy created and formed us. Genesis states that He used His energy to create us from dust taken from the ground.

Genesis 3:19
For dust, thou art, and unto dust shalt thou return.

God created us from His pure energy. His energy is stored in our body to help us. God's energy is unlimited so there is no lack of His help to get things done.

God provides help

The energy we have in us needs to be controlled. It must be at equilibrium otherwise we will be explosive like a bomb. Many times these forces may go out of balance, but God is always ready to help us restore the balance. Many of the lessons in the Bible spring from nature where shifts in balance are constantly taking place to reduce stress and to equalize the energies of life to create the beautiful life that God wants for us. We only have to observe a thunderstorm to see how these shifts in energy take place with the result being a sunny and fertile land. God is always there to help us through turbulent and stormy times and provide for us in an abundant way. We need to ask for help and He will generously provide it. As Matthew points out, God does much for the things He has created, even the simple flower, and He will do even more for us who He loves and created in His image and likeness.

Matthew 6:28-29
And why take ye thought for raiment? Consider the lilies of the field, how they grow; they toil not, neither do they spin: And yet I say unto you, that even Solomon in all his glory was not arrayed like one of these.

God does not create disorder and stress in either our personal or business lives. People through poor business and personal practices create stress. The role of the leader/manager is to remove stress through effective planning, delegation, and communications and to allow the free but balanced flow of employee energies to create and build an organization and business. Leaders who create an organization free from stress align themselves with God's will for His people. Leaders who do not create this environment are in conflict with the basic principles of nature. They cannot succeed in the end even though they are intelligent and technically skillful. The ancient leaders and Pharaohs of Egypt had great managers and engineers who could organize people and build the Pyramids. We herald these structures as great achievements and wonders of the world. Despite the achievements of the Pharaohs, their empire suffered grievously. Their actions toward people did not align with God's goals to treat people fairly, to treat them with respect, and to minimize their stress.

Treat people with respect

Exodus tells us how God harshly dealt with people who mistreated the Jewish workers during the Pharaoh's time. The Pharaoh's sufferings from the poor treatment of his workers should be a lesson to all of us. It shows how strongly God feels that we should align ourselves with His path and the fate that awaits leaders who do not. Exodus tells us how God eventually freed the Jews from their masters.

Exodus 1:11, 12:30-31
Therefore, they did set over them taskmasters to afflict them with their burdens. And they built for Pharaoh Treasure cities, Pithom and Raamses. And Pharaoh rose up in the night, he, and all his

servants, and all the Egyptians; and there was a great cry in Egypt for there was not a house where there was not one dead. And he called for Moses and Aaron by night, and said, Rise up, and get you forth from among my people, both ye and the children of Israel; and go, serve the Lord, as ye have said.

Leaders must remind themselves that in God's eyes we are all equal. That was a lesson the Pharaohs never learned. God gave us unique talents, and we have different roles to play in the world. The status or power we achieve in business does not make us any better than the lowest paid person in the organization in God's eyes. We can be caught up in the power and prestige of a position and forget this lesson. Luke reminds us that as leaders, we may be first in power and prestige but we may end up last at judgment.

Luke 13:30
And, behold, there are last which shall be first, and there are first which shall be last.

It is important that the leader not only "talk the talk" but also "walk the walk" when it comes to treating people equally and with respect. Leaders set the example by how they treat employees, and their actions echo throughout the organization. Matthew reminds us that we should not follow the example of leaders who do not do as they say.

Matthew 23:3-4
All therefore whatsoever they bid you observe and do: but do not ye after their works: for they say and do not. For they bind heavy burdens and grievous to be borne, and lay them on men's shoulders; but they themselves will not move them with one of their fingers.

If there is not fair treatment, a "them and us" mentally will prevail which will condemn the organization to mediocre status full of stressful discontent. James tells us that God sees no difference between rich and poor. James warns us not to discriminate by wealth or status because this is evil. A leader respects everyone.

> **James 2:2-5**
> For if there come unto your assembly a man with a gold ring, in goodly apparel, and there come in also a poor man in vile raiment; And ye have respect to him that weareth the gay clothing, and say unto him, Sit thou here in a good place; and say to the poor, Stand thou there, or sit here under my footstool: Are ye not then partial in yourselves, and are become judges of evil thoughts? Hearken, my beloved brethren, Hath not God chosen the poor of this world rich in faith, and heirs of the kingdom, which he hath promised to them, that love him?

We are of one spirit and purpose

Not everyone in business will be a leader or manage people, but we must all manage our personal lives effectively to achieve the peace and balance that God wills for families, friends, and us. St. Paul notes that each of us has a different role in the world, but we must all be of one spirit and purpose to achieve peace in our lives whether it is in a business or family environment.

> **1 Corinthians 12:4-7**
> Now there are diversities of gifts, but the same Spirit. And there are differences of administrations, but the same Lord. And there are diversities of operations, but it is the same God which worketh all in all. But the manifestation of the Spirit is given to every man to profit withal.

It takes work to manage both our public and private lives. It is not easy to be successful. Pressures and stresses face us daily. They come from family life problems, pressures at school and the work place. We cannot control these external stresses since we do not always get a choice. It is most important, however, that we control our personal emotions and stress levels to prevent anger and aggression that destroys the peace and harmony that God wants for us. Ecclesiastes tells us to control our emotions and not make hasty comments or take hasty actions that make us look the fool.

Ecclesiastes 7:9
Be not hasty in thy spirit to be angry: for anger resteth in the bosom of fools.

There are many techniques to help reduce personal stress like doing exercise, using a proper diet, creating a quiet reflective time each day, and getting proper rest. All these things help achieve a calm life. When events occur that can potentially bring stress, we need to be patient about what could happen or might happen in the future because of the event. Matthew tells us that worry does nothing to help the situation get resolved and that we should focus on today's issues. Do not agonize about the future over which we have little control.

Matthew 6:27, 34
Which of you by taking thought can add one cubit unto his stature? Take therefore no thought for the morrow: for the morrow shall take thought for the things of itself. Sufficient unto the day is the evil thereof.

It is better to focus our energy on positive ways to resolve or mitigate issues than to permit negative thoughts to grow in us. Negative thoughts drain energy and do not allow us to address problems effectively. Many a crisis we face today may seem like it is bringing about the end of life, as we know it. However, when we look back on the crises that occurred five years ago, in most cases, they do not seem to have been as tough to resolve or live through as we thought they were at the time. We need to have confidence that we can work things through with God's help. He has promised the faithful His help throughout the ages. Isaiah tells of us God's promise to His people.

Isaiah 41:10
Fear thou not; for I am with thee: be not dismayed; for I am thy God: I will strengthen thee; yea, I will help thee; yea, I will uphold thee with the right hand of my righteousness.

Learn and grow

With God's help, we can do things to minimize the stress that negative forces place on us, and the people we love. We help ourselves to accomplish this when we actively seek knowledge and educate ourselves. Proverbs emphasizes the need for us to seek wisdom and knowledge to gain peace. The wisdom we acquire has more value than gold and precious jewels.

Proverbs 3:13-18
Happy is the man that findeth wisdom, and the man that getteth understanding. For the merchandise of it is better than the merchandise of silver and the gain thereof than fine gold. She is more precious than rubies: and all the things thou canst desire are not to be compared unto her. Length of days is in her right hand; and in her left hand riches and honour. Her ways are ways of pleasantness, and all her paths are peace. She is a tree of life to them that lay hold upon her: and happy is every one that retaineth her.

Our Creator gives us special talents and He expects us to develop and use them for the good of all. In Exodus, we hear that He demands that we develop the talents given to us to do His work.

Exodus 35:10
And every wise-hearted among you shall come, and make all that the Lord hath commanded;

God rewards us when we work to develop the talents He has given us. We also have a responsibility to give both employees and family members the chance to grow, learn, and develop their God given talents. This is important to succeed in both our personal and business lives. However, training by itself is not enough. We must also use and test the skills learned to ensure competency.

Many employees who attend seminars praise the instructor and the class materials in post session questionnaires, but they rarely apply what they learned once they return to work. The main reason for this is that employees become too comfortable with old methods. They do not want to take a risk with the new methods. Changes in life can cause stress from fear of failure and most people just do not like change. As a result, people prefer to keep their old ways to ensure they get the work done and do not fail, even though the new methods may make their jobs easier and more efficient in the long run. We cannot place blame for not using new and more efficient methods solely on the employee. It is also a management problem! Management spends money to train people, sometimes millions of dollars, with the hope to get a return on the investment with improved efficiency. This money is often lost with no return on investment when management does not follow up on the application of the training.

Training must be practiced

Successful training programs have three steps. First, ensure the employee's supervisor understands and supports the training. Training can drive a wedge between the supervisor and the employee if the supervisor does not support or understand the training program. Supervisors should instruct attendees that they must apply what they learn. Supervisors need to set expectations before making the training investment. The seminar is not a holiday from work. Secondly, supervisors need to review the completed program with the employees to develop implementation plans. Thirdly, the supervisors need to do a follow up audit to see how the employees use the new knowledge and to see if there is improvement. If the results are not as expected, revise the training before others go through it and more money and time is wasted. No one would put money into an investment account and not check on the financial return, but more often than not, this is what happens with training investments, no one checks on results.

We need to practice leadership skills at home to improve our skills. Work with your children to create a vision for their future. Show them how education in their faith will help achieve that vision and give them a better life. Just as a business leader is responsible for the training of employees, parents must take responsibility to educate their children. Proverbs states that parents have a responsibility for their children's education.

Proverbs 22:6
Train up a child in the way he should go: and when he is old, he will not depart from it.

New methods require change and this can put stress on people already overloaded with work. They need support to be successful. Leadership can provide this support with additional resources during the training and implementation periods

In the work place, it is management's responsibility to schedule time, free from other duties, to let employees try new methods. Employees also need a work environment free from criticism and the fear of failure. Managers help employees find the time to try new methods when they assign additional help or permit the use of overtime work. The program organizer needs to put this cost into the budget and not assume the only cost is for class time. In the gospel of Matthew, he tells how a leader tests his employees during his absence to see what they have learned and how they apply it. The good performers get rewards, and he chastises poor performers.

Matthew 25:14-30
For the kingdom of heaven is as a man traveling into a far country, who called his own servants, and delivered unto them his goods. And unto one he gave five talents, to another two, and to another one; to every man according to his several ability; and straightway took his journey. Then he that had received the five talents went and traded with the same, and made them other five talents. And

likewise he that had received two, he also gained other two. But he that had received one went and digged in the earth, and hid his lord's money. After a long time the lord of those servants cometh, and reckoneth with them. And so he that had received five talents came and brought other five talents, saying, Lord, thou deliveredst unto me five talents: behold, I have gained beside them five talents more. His Lord said unto him, Well done, thou good and faithful servant: thou hast been faithful over a few things, I will make thee ruler over many things: enter thou into the joy of thy Lord. He also that had received two talents came and said, Lord, thou deliveredst unto me two talents: behold, I have gained two other talents beside them. His Lord said unto him, Well done, good and faithful servant; thou hast been faithful over a few things, I will make thee ruler over many things: enter thou into the joy of thy lord. Then he which had received the one talent came and said, Lord, I knew thee that thou art an hard man, reaping where thou hast not sown, and gathering where thou hast not strawed: And I was afraid, and went and hid thy talent in the earth: lo, there thou hast that is thine. His lord answered and said unto him, Thou wicked and slothful servant, thou knewest that I reap where I sowed not, and gather where I have not strawed: Thou oughtest therefore to have put my money to the exchangers, and then at my coming I should have received mine own with usury. Take therefore the talent from him, and give it unto him, which hath ten talents. For unto every one that hath shall be given, and he shall have abundance: but from him that hath not shall be taken away even that which he hath. And cast ye the unprofitable servant into outer darkness: there shall be weeping and gnashing of teeth.

Matthew's lesson is valuable. It reinforces the importance to test the skills we teach employees. It also points out that the servant who failed the test feared the wrath of his master and hence made the wrong decisions. This is a key point. It is the responsibility of leaders to drive out the fear of failure so that their employees feel free to take risks and make decisions at their level of responsibility. Employees and family members are like baseball or soccer players. They are never expected to play a perfect game and at times, they make errors. Tolerate failure during the learning period but review each failure. Discuss what positive lessons the employee learned from the failure and apply them to avoid future problems. This transforms a negative into a positive experience. The training review should not make employees feel they are the target of an inquisition. Patience is a virtue a leader needs to have to achieve the long-term benefit of training especially when things do not start well.

We have gifts to share

The sum total of all the talents given by God to the people of the world creates the means for societies to exist and flourish. Individuals seek out the things, which will fulfill and satisfy themselves. This creates a robust economy. It is truly amazing to stand back, look at the world, and observe how it works. People fill needed professions, in a field of thousands of professions, so that the world as a whole works efficiently. If God gave everyone the same talent, say to be only a violinist or machinist, the world, as we know it would not exist. Who would grow food, who would build houses and who would care for the sick? Instead, He has given us a variety of talents and abilities to ensure the world functions efficiently. Ephesians tells us that God has diversified and organized all labors to make a more loving world, and that the whole world is the sum of its many different parts.

> **Ephesians 4:15-16**
> But speaking the truth in love, may grow up into him in all things, which is the head, even Christ: From whom the whole body fitly joined together and compacted by that which every joint supplieth, according to the effectual working in the measure of every part, maketh increase of the body unto the edifying of itself in love.

It is God's plan that each of us helps our fellow brothers and sisters to satisfy their needs and help them lead a satisfying and rewarding life.

This brings satisfaction and fulfillment to our lives especially if we share the talents given to us with others. God expects us to use the talents He gave us and in doing so receive much more in return. We will find satisfaction if we follow the message in Paul's letters to the Thessalonians. He tells us to respect authority, appreciate the labors of others, and help the disadvantaged.

> **1 Thessalonians 5:12-15**
> And we beseech you, brethren, to know them which labour among you, and are over you in the Lord, and admonish you; And to esteem them very highly in love for their work's sake. And be at peace among yourselves. Now we exhort you, brethren, warn them that are unruly, comfort the feebleminded, support the weak, be patient toward all men. See that none render evil for evil unto any man; but ever follow that which is good, both among yourselves, and to all men.

Our journey and trials in life

When we are born, we start a great journey. Sometimes we are lucky to have a guiding light, a parent or friend, who influences us early on and helps us stay on the right path with only the occasional minor deviations. People who are not so fortunate may take the wrong path that leads into a spiral of despair, stress, and suffering. Matthew warns us that human fragility is a weakness that can lead to sin.

> **Matthew 26:41**
> Watch and pray that ye enter not into temptation: the spirit indeed is willing, but the flesh is weak.

We all seem to have an inherent ability to understand right from wrong, but that does not stop us from doing what is wrong. One might say in justification of a wrongful deed that we cannot understand what is good unless we also understand and experience what is not good. Whatever the reason, there are few of us who never stray from the right path. What is important is that God is all loving and forgiving! Like the loving father He is, He is always ready to forgive and take us back once we accept the right path of peace, love, and truth. We need to learn from mistakes, have the courage to make corrections and focus on the future, to make it better than the present or the past. Like the prodigal son, God always welcomes us back. Luke tells us how a loving father welcomed back his wayward son. Luke teaches us to have compassion for a family member and an employee who may wander from what is right but who return to the right path.

Luke 15:14-24
And when he had spent all, there arose a mighty famine in that land; and he began to be in want. And he went and joined himself to a citizen of that country; and he sent him into his fields to feed swine. And he would fain have filled his belly with the husks that the swine did eat: and no man gave unto him. And when he came to himself, he said, How many hired servants of my father's have bread enough and to spare, and I perish with hunger! I will arise and go to my father, and will say unto him, Father, I have sinned against heaven, and before thee, and am no more worthy to be called thy son: make me as one of thy hired servants. And he arose, and came to his father. But when he was yet a great way off, his father saw him, and had compassion, and ran, and fell on his neck, and kissed him. And the son said unto him, Father, I have sinned against heaven, and in thy sight, and am no more worthy to be called thy son. But the father said to his servants, Bring forth the best robe, and put it on him; and put a ring on his hand, and shoes on his feet: And bring hither the fatted calf, and kill it; and let us eat, and be merry: For this my son was dead, and is alive again; he was lost, and is found. And they began to be merry.

We can create a better environment with less stress for employees placed in our care but first we must look inward. Our beliefs must value the lives of others over our personal ambitions. We need to accept our weaknesses and continually relearn and reinvent ourselves to work toward a state of perfection by practicing the lessons we learn. As humans, we will never achieve perfection, but the path we follow to achieve perfection will bring us a peace and satisfaction that is God's reward on earth. John teaches that baptism by water and the Spirit is necessary to gain God's reward. We are sinners. If we are on the wrong path, we need to reinvent ourselves by changing the beliefs that put us on the wrong path, and be born again to achieve God's kingdom.

John 3:4-7
Nicodemus saith unto him, How can a man be born when he is old? Can he enter the second time into his mother's womb, and be born? Jesus answered, Verily, verily, I say unto thee, Except a man be born of water and of the Spirit, he cannot enter into the kingdom of God. That which is born of the flesh is flesh; and that which is born of the Spirit is spirit. Marvel not that I said unto thee, Ye must be born again.

Discipline is a virtue we need to have to be true to the lessons of the prophets, to hold fast to the leadership principles they teach, and not to allow ourselves to stray with each new leadership style fad that comes along. We need to stay the course, even when others criticize us as being backward because we do not accept trendy ideas. Isaiah gives us a lesson how to be strong and steadfast in the face of opposition, despite the suffering we endure, for God will be there to help us and vanquish people who punish us.

Isaiah 50:5-9
The Lord God hath opened mine ear, and I was not rebellious, neither turned away back. I gave my back to the smiters, and my cheeks to them that plucked off the hair: I hid not my face from shame and spitting. For the Lord God will help me; therefore shall I not be confounded: therefore have I set my face like a flint, and

I know that I shall not be ashamed. He is near that justifieth me; who will contend with me? Let us stand together: who is mine adversary? Let him come near to me. Behold, the Lord God will help me; who is he that shall condemn me? Lo, they all shall wax old as a garment; the moth shall eat them up.

Part 2 – Take the Bible's lessons to work

Introduction

In Part 2, the focus is on applying the Bible's lessons to specific leadership topics to help us to be successful and at the same time to achieve harmony in life. God wants to help us to be successful and to be without sin. We commit sin when we miss the targets God set for us. The word sin comes from the Aramaic word *khatatha* that refers to an archer who misses the target. A servant shouted the word to let the archer know he missed the mark and the archer should try again. Leaders have multiple targets they must hit to achieve success. Critics are always quick to tell us when we miss a target. A financial target missed is a small sin compared to not aligning ourselves with God's targets of peace, love, and truth. Biblical lessons help us to reassess when we miss a target and encourage us to try again. We have a forgiving God who is always ready to let us take another shot at the target.

Leadership Topics

Management by walking around

God gave us guidance in the Bible through His prophets. They foretold the coming of Christ. Christ came into the world to experience every aspect of life, both joyful and sad. God did not keep His son on a lofty throne on earth out of touch with people. He sent Him to walk with His people who He will someday judge. Matthew describes Christ's journeys and His personal contacts with the people.

> **Matthew 4:23-25**
> And Jesus went about all Galilee, teaching in their synagogues, and preaching the gospel of the kingdom, and healing all manner of sickness and all manner of disease among the people. And his fame went throughout all Syria: and they brought unto him all sick people that were taken with divers diseases and torments, and those, which were possessed with devils, and those, which were lunatick, and those that had the palsy; and he healed them. And there followed him great multitudes of people from Galilee, and from Decapolis, and from Jerusalem, and from Judaea, and from beyond Jordan.

Managers who stay in their office and think they understand what is going on in their organization can learn from Christ's example. Management by walking around is a key to success. Like Christ, we must have personal contact with people to help them with issues, to instruct them on what they need to know, and to gain first hand insight into the alignment of their work with the strategies of the organization. Walk around and see if the business' plans, strategies, and goals are actually taking root in the organization. This is not difficult to do. A great time to meet with associates and get feedback is at coffee breaks or at luncheon roundtables. Do not immediately launch into business topics. Start a conversation by asking about each person's backgrounds and hobbies. This is a great opportunity to learn about your employees' backgrounds and their hidden personal talents. The conversation will often drift to business topics as the employees probe for information of interest to them.

It may be impossible to make contact with every person in a large corporation, but a manager can do a large enough sampling to see what is going on. Unfortunately, many managers find excuses why they do not have time to walk around. They are not doing their job and will not be successful in the end. It takes commitment, planning, and energy to get out of the office. Many leaders and managers unfortunately do not possess these disciplines even though they need them. In Hebrews, we learn that Jesus walked among us and was tempted as we are tempted. He has compassion for us and He will help us overcome our temptations. Leaders who walk around and understand their associates, and the world they live in, are better able to help them. A leader who knows his associates on a personal base will be more compassionate. All of us share human frailty so a leader who understands his own frailty will have more compassion for others. The passage from Hebrews reminds us of this truth.

Hebrews 2:18
For in that he himself hath suffered being tempted, he is able to succour them that are tempted.

Because a manager cannot be everywhere, it is important to train subordinates to get feedback. Subordinates can do this work if their leaders provide training to both communicate the right message and be a good listener. Without help and delegation, a leader will quickly falter. Christ gives us a lesson in Luke on how to spread vision and strategy messages through delegation. He appoints and instructs seventy disciples in addition to His twelve to go in pairs, as a team, to proclaim His words across the nations. He also notes it will not be easy since there will be difficult people, the wolves, to deal with who will want to protect their turf against change. Train disciples to spread the word of change and prepare them to deal with the wolves.

Luke 10:1-3
After these things the Lord appointed other seventy also, and sent them two and two before his face into every city and place, whither he himself would come. Therefore said he unto them, the harvest truly is great, but the labourers are few: pray ye therefore the Lord of the harvest that he would send forth labourers into his harvest. Go your ways: behold, I send you forth as lambs among wolves.

New technology has made spreading information easier. Online web meetings, which are now affordable and user friendly, can minimize the need for travel, but technology should never entirely replace face-to-face interaction. Matthew encourages us to become a seeker of knowledge by personal contact with people. A reward, as Matthew points out, is the recognition and admiration of the people who appreciate the chance to have a conversation with their leader. The message also notes that once people know that help is available, they will seek it out to improve themselves and in doing so improve the entire business. Nothing is worse for morale than people who feel isolated and do not come forward for help because they do not believe their leadership has a personal interest in them. People who do not seek help to solve problems will unwittingly destroy an organization. Groups within the organization will become demoralized and inefficient if help is not there to clear roadblocks to progress that they cannot clear by themselves. Matthew gives us the words a leader needs to communicate as a personal commitment to provide help. The result will be a workforce committed to follow the leader as people followed Christ because He did good works for them.

<u>Matthew 7:7-8</u>
Ask, and it shall be given you; seek, and ye shall find; knock, and it shall be opened unto you: For every one that asketh receiveth; and he that seeketh findeth; and to him that knocketh it shall be opened.

Be proactive

We have the gift of free will. The outcomes of the ventures we make in life, whether of a personal or business nature, are dependent on what we do to achieve what we desire. There are two choices. The choice is ours to either let things happen as they may and hope the outcomes are satisfactory and pleasing to us, or to be more proactive, and direct our activities and energies to ensure we will more likely achieve the things that bring us satisfaction. The proactive approach takes more energy and work but the likelihood of a positive outcome is greatly increased. James tells us that we should be proactive and be a doer.

James 1:22
But be ye doers of the word, and not hearers only, deceiving your own selves.

To achieve satisfaction in life, it is necessary to understand what we want and why it is important. Second, we must determine the steps needed to achieve the result. A cardinal rule is to be careful what you ask of God because you might get it. Sometimes we crave a certain thing in life to make us happy, but when we get it, we end up being worse off than before. The best day in many boaters' lives is the day they take delivery of a new boat. The second best day for many is when they sell the boat after they realize they have a hole in the water in which they are pouring thousands of dollars and hundreds of hours of maintenance. Leaders need to keep a conversation alive with God and make it a part of their daily activities to ask for God's guidance. Who better to give leaders advice about what they need in life than the One who knows all things? James reminds us to talk with God and He will surely help us to find what we need.

James 1:5
If any of you lack wisdom, let him ask of God, that gives to all men liberally, and upbraided not; and it shall be given him.

We can help ourselves by devoting time to carefully examining the ramifications of the outcomes we desire to ensure that we really want to live with these results in the long term. If you really like running a small business, do you want to grow large despite the potential financial rewards? What outcome are you looking for, money, or internal satisfaction? Whatever the final desires we wish to fulfill, we must have faith that these things will happen with God's help. As Matthew points out, faith and prayer are the keys to achieve what will make us happy in life.

Matthew 21:21-22
Jesus answered and said unto them, Verily I say unto you, If ye have faith, and doubt not, ye shall not only do this which is done

to the fig tree, but also if ye shall say unto this mountain, Be thou removed, and be thou cast into the sea; it shall be done. In addition, all things, whatsoever ye shall ask in prayer, believing, ye shall receive.

When, despite the most sincere prayers, self-examination, and faith we do not get what we want, we should not be anxious with God or remorseful. We must trust that whatever it was we wanted was not right for us at the time. It may not be obvious today but years out in hindsight, it will be clear that what happened was for the best. A promotion not received, but which may have increased business travel time may be a blessing. Many marriages fail or significant family child problems develop because travel separation brings stress to the family. God knows what is best for us and gives us what we need to be happy in the end. Looking back over a thirty-eight year working career, events that seemed to be have been a terrible let down at the time proved to be right thing in the end. Luke tells us that God listens to us.

Luke 11:9-13
If a son shall ask bread of any of you that is a father, will he give him a stone? Or if he ask a fish, will he for a fish give him a serpent? Or if he shall ask an egg, will he offer him a scorpion? If ye then, being evil, know how to give good gifts unto your children: how much more shall your heavenly Father give the Holy Spirit to them that ask him?

Learn from the master planner
Genesis lets us see how God went about His work proactively as the ultimate leader to create a new enterprise, the world. This is an example we should follow. God did not let things happen by chance. He followed a carefully laid out plan to achieve a world, as He wanted it to be. Careful thought and reflection went into each part of the creation. It teaches us that the success of a venture results from close attention to the details. When we read Genesis, we see that God reflects back on the work He did at each

step to ensure a solid foundation before He proceeded to the next step. It is an example every leader should follow.

Genesis 1:1-12

In the beginning, God created the heaven and the earth. And the earth was without form, and void; and darkness was upon the face of the deep. And the Spirit of God moved upon the face of the waters. And God said, Let there be light: and there was light. And God saw the light, that it was good: and God divided the light from the darkness. And God called the light Day, and the darkness he called Night. And the evening and the morning were the first day. And God said, Let there be a firmament in the midst of the waters, and let it divide the waters from the waters. And God made the firmament, and divided the waters, which were under the firmament from the waters, which were above the firmament: and it was so. And God called the firmament Heaven. And the evening and the morning were the second day. And God said, Let the waters under the heaven be gathered together unto one place, and let the dry land appear: and it was so. And God called the dry land Earth; and the gathering together of the waters called the Seas: and God saw that it was good. And God said, Let the earth bring forth grass, the herb yielding seed, and the fruit tree yielding fruit after his kind, whose seed is in itself, upon the earth: and it was so. And the earth brought forth grass and herb yielding seed after his kind, and the tree yielding fruit, whose seed was in itself, after his kind: and God saw that it was good.

This scripture is a good business plan example. It had clear objectives and a time-based plan of six days to get things done in an orderly manner. God teaches us the importance to make plans. We will accomplish the most when we plan. Conversely, the lack of a plan will result in a low success rate. He also gave us a lesson in Genesis that all work and no rest is a bad thing. Again, this emphasizes the balance we must achieve between work and leisure to gain the peace God wants for us on this earth.

Genesis 2:1-3
Thus the heavens and the earth were finished, and all the host of them. And on the seventh day God ended his work which he had made; and he rested on the seventh day from all his work, which he had made. And God blessed the seventh day, and sanctified it: because that in it he had rested from all his work, which God created and made.

Genesis clearly shows the world did not just happen. God was proactive and even though He was attentive to details, He kept focus on the major events He planned to accomplish each day. Good leaders know to focus on the important elements in their plan and not get lost in non-value added tasks that waste time and money. Ecclesiastes reminds us to avoid getting lost in a myriad of tasks. It is important to prioritize tasks and accomplish a few important things or we will be disappointed and frustrated.

Ecclesiastes 4:6
Better is a handful with quietness, than both the hands full with travail and vexation of spirit.

Know your sheep
Leaders seek to understand the people they deal with whether they are an employee, customer or family member. We understand people better when we walk around and get to know them personally. As John notes, a good leader knows and calls his followers by name.

John 10:3-4
To him the porter openeth; and the sheep hear his voice: and he calleth his own sheep by name, and leadeth them out. And when he putteth forth his own sheep, he goeth before them, and the sheep follow him: for they know his voice.

John's message tells us it is important to get background knowledge of our associates. Many times a one on one meeting reveals an associate's hidden talents and abilities that can help the organization. Leaders also need to understand their customers on a personal basis to ensure that the customers get what they need in products and services. Employees and customers will be faithful and work hard for a helpful person they know and trust.

Face-to-face contact seems to get more difficult with each new advance in communication technology. In an age of electronic communication, it is easy to shoot off emails, text messages, leave voicemails, and send faxes. These are necessary tools today, but they have drawbacks. Unfortunately, people use emails so the sender does not have to look the other person in the eye and deal with emotions. They use emails to drop bombs on rivals. They do not see or hear the person attacked. A one-on-one conversation brings a dimension of emotional exchange that can reveal the true comfort or displeasure someone has with your thoughts. Observing body language is a great tool to understand whether there is agreement or disagreement during the conversation. A face-to-face conversation is the best approach to understand a person's feelings, but it takes a brave person with emotional strength to do it.

John talks in the following passages about the importance for followers to know their leader. He warns about the delegation of responsibility to others in the organization, the hireling, who may not have the same dedication to the employees and customers and who might falter under stress. This teaches us that we need to give associates a stake or ownership in the business to ensure that the business is a priority in their lives so they will not falter when things get tough. Many companies have stock award plans to ensure the employees have ownership in the business to motivate them and guide their thoughts. In modern times, the wolf at the door that might frighten a hireling can be financial or personal problems, political infighting, or fear of failure in the business. These things can cause the focus and purpose of the business to be lost. John's gospel describes the traits a good leader needs to develop so he is not a stranger to his flock.

John 10:5-15
And a stranger will they not follow, but will flee from him: for they know not the voice of strangers. This parable spake Jesus unto them: but they understood not what things they were which he spake unto them. Then said Jesus unto them again, Verily, verily, I say unto you, I am the door of the sheep. All that ever came before me are thieves and robbers: but the sheep did not hear them. I am the door: by me if any man enters in, he shall be saved, and shall go in and out, and find pasture. The thief cometh not, but for to steal, to kill, and to destroy: I am come that they might have life, and that they might have it more abundantly. I am the good shepherd: the good shepherd giveth his life for the sheep. But he that is a hireling, and not the shepherd, whose own the sheep are not, seeth the wolf coming, and leaveth the sheep, and fleeth: and the wolf catcheth them, and scattereth the sheep. The hireling fleeth, because he is a hireling, and careth not for the sheep. I am the good shepherd, and know my sheep, and am known of mine. As the Father knoweth me, even so know I the Father: and I lay down my life for the sheep.

Business leaders have the responsibility to provide a more abundant life for their associates, family, and themselves. There have been too many examples over the years of thieves, in the disguise of trusted leaders, who extract what they can from the organization for personal gain at the expense of others. We have seen the tyranny of these thieves in recent times in the stock market. They were the ones who ran Ponzi schemes for their personal benefit. When the schemes failed, they destroyed both the personal lives of their investors, charitable institutions who invested with them and the people the institutions helped. These thieves worked contrary to God's design and it led to their eventual downfall and disgrace. The suffering of people who commit these crimes is not limited to the criminal punishment and personal disgraces of the here and now. Amos warns us that God will not forget the deeds of people who are deceitful towards others or direct their priorities to gain wealth at the expense of others. One can only imagine the wrath to befall dishonest people whose actions make the poor suffer even more.

Amos 8:4-7
Hear this, O ye that swallow up the needy, even to make the poor of the land to fail, Saying, When will the new moon be gone, that we may sell corn? And the Sabbath, that we may set forth wheat, making the ephah small, and the shekel great, and falsifying the balances by deceit? That we may buy the poor for silver, and the needy for a pair of shoes; yea, and sell the refuse of the wheat? The Lord hath sworn by the excellency of Jacob, Surely I will never forget any of their works.

St. Paul builds upon Amos's warning by reminding us that each of us should treat people we care for with honesty and respect, since each of us has a boss in heaven who we must eventually answer too.

Colossians 4:1
Masters, give unto your servants that which is just and equal; knowing that ye also have a Master in heaven.

Reduce stress
One way to treat people well is to help them reduce the impact of stress in their lives. Stress is an enemy that can weaken a productive and enthusiastic work force. The leader's role is to help reduce stress to keep people productive today and to remain productive over the long run. There is nothing more unproductive and dangerous than employees who lack focus in their work because their minds are churning through other issues. Stress from a recent divorce, financial troubles, or a critical family issue may weigh heavily on a person's mind and cause that person not to give full attention to the work. This can lead to serious accidents, especially around machinery, when associates' minds are off in space while their hands are near moving machine parts. Alternatively, if they drive a car and do not focus on their surroundings, they can cause an accident. How

many times have we arrived at the end of a car trip and realized we were not attentive during the trip because we were lost in thought. Stress can cause sick people to fear the loss of their job if they are recovering at home. Consequently, they may rush back to work before they are completely healthy and infect other workers.

The leader needs to seek out and pay careful attention to associates who may be under stress and provide them help to ensure they can do their job safely. This includes associates who are in poor health and may infect others. Supervisors need training to recognize the signs of these issues and, if necessary, counsel the employees, reassign them to safer work, or send them home to recover fully from a sickness. Employees should feel free to discuss issues with management that may affect their performance without fear of reprisal. Work schedules must ensure employees have sufficient time to rest during the workday and during the workweek. Rest promotes clear thought and efficiency. Overtime work is often necessary to handle peak workloads but experience dictates that if overtime goes on for too long, productivity is lost. Employee fatigue will cause output to decrease and waste the overtime money. In other words, you pay for ten hours work but only get eight hours of value because the employee is fatigued and this slows the pace. Often employees will not complain of fatigue or stress because they like the overtime salary, but output will diminish with time.

Jesus recognized the hard work of His disciples and took the initiative to have them rest because He could see they were near exhaustion. Mark relates the care Jesus took of the apostles.

<u>Mark 6:30-31</u>
And the apostles gathered themselves together unto Jesus, and told him all things, both what they had done, and what they had taught. And he said unto them, Come ye yourselves apart into a desert place, and rest a while: for there were many coming and going, and they had no leisure so much as to eat.

The leader also plays an important role to shield his followers from organizational induced stress. This stress can come from corporate pressure, external sources, or from direct superiors who are overly aggressive or obtrusive in their demands. The leader needs to handle these issues and not pass them verbatim to the employees without first translating aggressive or abusive language into more civil terms. Most employees have enough issues to worry about in their day-to-day jobs without additional concerns placed upon them that they have no way to influence. Jesus sets an example for protecting associates when He shields the disciples from the soldiers who confronted Him in the garden at Gethsemane. The soldiers then led Him away for trial and execution. John tells us that Jesus was able to protect and shield all His disciples and did not lose even one.

John 18:7-9
Then asked he them again, Whom seek ye? And they said, Jesus of Nazareth. Jesus answered, I have told you that I am he: if therefore ye seek me, let these go their way: That the saying might be fulfilled, which he spake, Of them which thou gavest me have I lost none.

Communicate effectively

Leaders appeal to our emotions with messages that energize and inspire. The inspiration we receive moves us to action. Effective leaders help us over personal roadblocks and they get us to do what we know we should do, but for various reasons, we find difficult to initiate or complete. We need this push at times to be more productive with the talents that God has given to us. Jeremiah tells us that God will reward us in proportion to the efforts we make to earn the reward.

Jeremiah 17:10
I the Lord search the heart; I try the reins, even to give every man according to his ways, and according to the fruit of his doings.

Communications that inspire are therefore critical to the development and delivery of a business plan. They are necessary not only to give out information but also to receive information and feedback from associates and customers to fine tune plans. The leader needs to connect needs from potential customers with the resources and skills of the organization and its extended family of suppliers and service providers. Patient communications can achieve this. We find, however, that communication is not easy for many and most of us lack communication skills. The greatest fear most people have is to stand before a crowd and make a speech let alone one that is inspirational. We need to ask God's help with communications since it is often hard to find the right words to inspire others. Isaiah tells us that God will provide words for us when we have righteous intentions and He will watch over us.

Isaiah 51:16
And I have put my words in thy mouth, and I have covered thee in the shadow of mine hand, that I may plant the heavens, and lay the foundations of the earth, and say unto Zion, Thou art my people.

Seek experienced guidance

People promoted to leadership positions must undergo a change in their mental image of themselves. As workers, they execute orders, and for this work, they receive rewards. Workers often get promotions solely because they are competent in their current jobs. Workers may have expert technical skills and get along with their peers. However, if they lack the essential skill of communications, management should not promote them. As a leader, one must prepare the path for others and provide direction, and this requires communication skills. There is an entirely different mindset required to lead that is not easy for many to adopt, especially after years of taking instruction, and not giving instruction. The Bible reminds us that we must change as we mature, create ourselves anew, and replace old ways with new ways.

1 Corinthians 13:11
When I was a child, I spake as a child, I understood as a child, I thought as a child: but when I became a man, I put away childish things.

Leaders need to seek out the wisdom and guidance of experienced people to help establish direction for themselves and to learn business procedures. These business advisors can act as an informal or formal Board of Directors that brings specific expertise to the business. In family life, these advisors are sometimes the parents, grandparents, uncles, aunts or religious pastors whose wisdom and success over the years have earned them respect for good advice. Not respecting the advice of people who have the experience and the wisdom that comes with time, has led to the downfall of many leaders. As we see in the message from Kings, King Rehoboam of Judah sought advice from experienced advisors, the community elders.

1 Kings 12:6-7
And king Rehoboam consulted with the old men that stood before Solomon his father while he yet lived, and said, How do ye advise that I may answer this people? And they spake unto him, saying, If thou wilt be a servant unto this people this day, and wilt serve them, and answer them, and speak good words to them, then they will be thy servants forever.

Unfortunately, King Rehoboam did not follow the advice of these wise advisors. He paid the price paid by most vanquished leaders, the loss of his followers and kingdom. Many leaders disregard the wisdom of age and experience for younger and trendy ideas, which have not withstood the test of time yet sound appealing. That is not to say we should ignore new ideas. A leader has to weigh both the sage advice of experienced advisors and people who suggest new ideas and technologies. A wise leader tests out new ideas on a small scale before going full out with them. As we see in the message from Kings, King Rehoboam went full out with the untested ideas of his youthful followers and lost.

1 Kings 12:8, 13, 18
But he forsook the counsel of the old men, which they had given him, and consulted with the young men that were grown up with

him, and which stood before him: And the king answered the people roughly, and forsook the old men's counsel that they gave him; Then king Rehoboam sent Adoram, who was over the tribute; and all Israel stoned him with stones, that he died. Therefore, king Rehoboam made speed to get him up to his chariot, to flee to Jerusalem.

Leaders must delegate to succeed

To implement a plan, a great amount of labor is required to develop detailed strategies and complimentary objectives to include short-term goals and timelines. Delegation of responsibility provides the hours of help to get the work done. Exodus explains to us that failure to delegate can overburden and wear out the leader. This is especially true in charitable organizations where a few people carry the burden for lack of volunteers. In the home, delegation of duties to each family member relieves the stress on parents and especially on single parents. Delegation spreads the work to lighten the burden on each person and prevent burn out. In Exodus, we hear Moses's father-in-law give him advice to reduce his leadership burden by delegating work to a large, organized group of people.

> **Exodus 18:18-21**
> Thou wilt surely wear away, both thou, and this people that is with thee: for this thing is too heavy for thee; thou art not able to perform it thyself alone. Hearken now unto my voice, I will give thee counsel, and God shall be with thee: Be thou for the people to Godward, that thou mayest bring the causes unto God: And thou shalt teach them ordinances and laws, and shalt shew them the way wherein they must walk, and the work that they must do. Moreover thou shall provide out of all the people able men, such as fear God, men of truth, hating covetousness; and place such over them, to be rulers of thousands, and rulers of hundreds, rulers of fifties and rulers of tens.

People are reluctant to accept delegation or trust a leader they do not know. However, people are willing to work for leaders who demonstrate that they are intelligent, energetic, respectful of others, and have a clear vision for the future. These traits are far more important to people than the leader's position, title, or wealth. We earn respect with straightforward and honest personal dealings. Associates who get respect return it, which forms a strong bond. The most difficult time to show respect is when someone needs correction after a small disaster. Leaders need to keep cool and not publicly criticize a person or group in an attempt to change behavior, or they are doomed to fail and to lose respect. Matthew gives us good advice on how a leader should counsel associates to achieve their respect and loyalty. In addition, Matthew tells us that Christ expects us to show patience and forgiveness.

Matthew 18:15, 21-22
Moreover, if thy brother shall trespass against thee, go and tell him his fault between thee and him alone: if he shall hear thee, thou hast gained thy brother. Then came Peter to him, and said, Lord, how oft shall my brother sin against me, and I forgive him? Till seven times? Jesus saith unto him, I say not unto thee, Until seven times: but, Until seventy times seven.

Team members have responsibilities
Associates have an obligation to be loyal and faithful to the leader, the head of the organization, and their fellow employees even when they do not fully agree with them. Matthew tells us that we need to respect the leaders at home and work. In turn, leaders need to be servants to the people they lead.

Matthew 19:19, 20:27
Honour thy father and thy mother: and, Thou shalt love thy neighbour as thyself. And whosoever will be chief among you, let him be your servant:

One of the squabbling points employees often dwell on is their pay. This is especially true if they feel someone in the group, whom they think is not as talented or as hard working, gets more compensation. In Matthew's gospel, the Lord is clear that we should be satisfied with what compensation we agree to and not mumble or complain.

Matthew 20:8-16
So when even was come, the lord of the vineyard saith unto his steward, Call the labourers, and give them their hire, beginning from the last unto the first. And when they came that were hired about the eleventh hour, they received every man a penny. But when the first came, they supposed that they should have received more; and they likewise received every man a penny. And when they had received it, they murmured against the goodman of the house, Saying, These last have wrought but one hour, and thou hast made them equal unto us, which have borne the burden and heat of the day. But he answered one of them, and said, Friend, I do thee no wrong: didst not thou agree with me for a penny? Take that thine is, and go thy way: I will give unto this last, even as unto thee. Is it not lawful for me to do what I will with mine own? Is thine eye evil, because I am good? So the last shall be first, and the first last: for many be called, but few chosen.

When we accept compensation, we should do the best job possible to live up to the contract we made when we accepted employment. Likewise, we expect employers to live up to their end of the contract. In Matthew, Jesus tells us to give what is due to our employer.

Matthew 22:19-21
Shew me the tribute money. And they brought unto him a penny. And he saith unto them, Whose is this image and superscription? They say unto him, Caesar's. Then saith he unto them, Render therefore unto Caesar the things which are Caesar's; and unto God the things that are God's.

Leaders have responsibilities to society

Great leaders achieve greatness through their actions. However, their success would not have been possible without God's guidance and help. We repay this help by being good stewards of the world's resources. Luke tells us that we need to be humble because the gifts we are given are so marvelous.

> **Luke 14:11**
> For whosoever exalteth himself shall be abased; and he that humbleth himself shall be exalted.

The plan that drives the organization forward must respect the equality of everyone in society so that it does not encroach on the rights and freedoms of others. This includes the right to a clean environment and good health. In Genesis, God gives us the command to use the earth and its resources for everyone's benefit. He also admonishes us to be good stewards of the earth, "to dress it and keep it." The earth is a gift we should not abuse for the sake of profit or convenience. We need to care for it and replenish what we take to sustain it for future generations.

> **Genesis 2:15**
> And the Lord God took the man, and put him into the Garden of Eden to dress it and to keep it.

A business should not seek a benefit in a way that harms others. High standards for health and safety should apply not only to associates but also to customers and neighbors. Great leaders strive for the highest standards even though local regulations and practices may be lenient or even non-existent. This is especially true in emerging nations where regulations may be lower than U.S. standards. In these countries, people are at a disadvantage. Treat people worldwide equally with a uniform level of respect, care, and fairness. It is not only the law of the land we should fear if we harm the earth and its peoples but also the wrath of God if we abuse what He created. Ephesians tells us that we are all fellow citizens in God's household.

Ephesians 2:19
Now therefore ye are no more strangers and foreigners, but fellow citizens with the saints, and of the household of God.

Treat competitors fairly and do not use unlawful methods to defeat them. Respect includes truthfulness in business dealings and with the competition. Do not use a competitor's confidential information for your advantage. Laws in many countries mandate compliance to fair business practices. Many leaders set out written compliance guidelines to ensure overzealous associates do not violate fair practices and subject the entire organization to ridicule and loss of respect in the community. One violation in a small part of the organization, or by a single person, can shed a bad light on the entire organization. We saw this in a dramatic way when U.S. companies were found using child labor in their foreign production facilities. The bad publicity was enormous and cost the companies the reputation and sales they had spent millions of dollars to build up. Deuteronomy tells us that honest businesses do not covet or use things that do not belong to them.

Deuteronomy 5:20-21
Neither shalt thou bear false witness against thy neighbour. Neither shalt thou desire thy neighbour's wife, neither shalt thou covet thy neighbour's house, his field, or his manservant, or his maidservant, his ox, or his ass, or anything that is thy neighbour's.

Customs and cultures are as important to understand as the laws and regulations of the places were business is done. Legal departments usually research laws and regulations when a business ventures into a new part of the country or a foreign land, but they typically do not do research to understand local customs and culture. This can lead to disastrous results. We live in a world where insults to cultural or religious standards can close a market to our products. For instance, there are very specific formalities to adhere to when meeting new business people in Japan. Businesswomen adhere to strict dress standards in the Middle East to avoid problems.

One country may allow certain food ingredients, but another country may ban them. Fortunately, most business people are tolerant of cultural mistakes newcomers make. However, it shows respect when we research and understand local customs. This gives a much more positive impression to new business partners since respect for their customs shows respect for them. In Romans, we hear that we honor others when we honor their customs.

Romans 13:7
Render therefore to all their dues: tribute to whom tribute is due; custom to whom custom; fear to whom fear; honour to whom honour.

Communicate performance and compliance practices to the organization in a clear manner to ensure the practices are part of the daily work ethic. Everyone must understand and abide by all laws and norms to avoid harmful negative publicity. Some good advice to follow when making a decision is to see that decision as a headline in the local newspaper. If the decision does not make a good headline, you are making the wrong decision. Always assume whatever you say or do will be a headline. Paul in his letter to the Colossians reminds us that what we cast out on the water will return to us.

Colossians 3:25
But he that doeth wrong shall receive for the wrong, which he hath done: and there is no respect of persons.

The Bible teaches us to be proactive, to listen attentively, to create a vision, and to develop a strong team. It also emphasizes that leaders should lead and teach by example because our actions speak louder than words. Jesus validates this as He often taught the disciples with actions first and then words. In John's gospel, he describes how Jesus first washed the feet of the disciples to show them by example that they had to be servants to the people. He then explained His actions. Communicate annually the principles that drive the organization as the church repeats scripture passages every year to guide us.

John 13:13-16
Ye call me Master and Lord: and ye say well; for so I am. If I then, your Lord and Master, have washed your feet; ye also ought to wash one another's feet. For I have given you an example, that ye should do as I have done to you. Verily, verily, I say unto you, The servant is not greater than his lord; neither he that is sent greater than he that sent him.

Good leaders create good organizations when their positive and respectful actions reflect down through the chain of command and set an example for their subordinates. Corrupt leaders create a corrupt organization through disrespectful actions. These leaders fail with time.

Matthew 12:33
Either makes the tree good, and his fruit good; or else make the tree corrupt, and his fruit corrupt: for the tree is known by his fruit.

Leaders have to accomplish many things to move their organization forward. They have a responsibility to learn and to practice leadership skills, but hard work should not preclude having fun. One of my fondest memories from my Canadian experience was a call I received from the packaging department manager. She informed me that the factory manager always played Santa Claus and handed out grab bag gifts to the packaging employees at their Christmas luncheon in the cafeteria. It was not in my list of leadership practice priorities, but it was fun playing Santa.

Vision and Strategy Development

A leader has to set the direction for the business and get all the stakeholders involved and committed to it.

Build your vision for the future

The components for a good business plan include a stated purpose for the enterprise, a vision for the future, strategies with clear long and short-term objectives and a statement of the values that will govern conduct as we proceed forward. These building blocks provide direction and knowledge to the entire organization. Proverbs stresses the need to build a business based on knowledge supported by both fact-finding research and experience.

> **Proverbs 24:3-5**
> Through wisdom is a house builded; and by understanding it is established: And by knowledge shall the chambers be filled with all precious and pleasant riches. A wise man is strong; yea, a man of knowledge increaseth strength.

Understanding the purpose of the business we are in is a first step in the preparation of a business plan. If you are a baker, ask yourself if the business is limited to making bread or making a range of products. Define the scope of the business. Do you want to be a niche business or a global business? For instance, a purpose might be, "we make baked goods for distribution in our city." Try to select the words to describe the business purpose that do not constrain future growth ideas. The purpose should not be too broad or too narrow. A narrow purpose statement may limit thoughts and ideas for future growth prospects. Many businesses start small and local, and with success, they expand. We minimize risk when the business scope is limited at the start while expertise and markets are developed. However, always keep an eye open to future opportunity

Elements of a strong vision statement

A written vision statement is an important step to complete a business plan. The vision addresses in simple terms what the organization wants to achieve. It provides overall direction and clarifies the business purpose without the clutter of too many details or financial numbers. Vision wording must not restrict future growth by being too narrow in scope. The vision is the banner around which the associates will rally. It forms the base from which to build strategies, and it provides a guideline for daily actions. A simple vision statement for a bakery might be, "we create and produce premium priced baked goods for special occasions which are known for their originality of design and memorable quality and taste."

A well-written vision statement energizes associates to be creative and to work to make the business a success. It is most effective when it is able to appeal to the associates on an emotional level since this will increase their resolve to make the business a success. Many organizations use catchy words or phrases that can help people recall the nature and substance of the vision. A worldwide delivery service may put words in a vision statement like "worldwide overnight and we get it right" to indicate the importance to deliver parcels overnight anywhere in the world with a high level of customer satisfaction. Nehemiah tells us how a single leader used vision to communicate, energize, and rally his followers to build a protective wall in Jerusalem.

> **Nehemiah 2:17-18**
> Then said I unto them, Ye see the distress that we are in, how Jerusalem lieth waste, and the gates thereof are burned with fire: come, and let us build up the wall of Jerusalem, that we be no more a reproach. Then I told them of the hand of my God, which was good upon me; as also the king's words that he had spoken unto me. And they said, Let us rise up and build. So they strengthened their hands for this good work.

Nehemiah shared his vision to make Jerusalem a safe place. The vision had the intrinsic support of the people since who would not want to be safe in their home city. The appeal to their emotions to save their families and homes encouraged strong participation. Nehemiah had confidence in the skills of his people, but he had to push them toward the goal. The challenge gave the people the energy to participate in the vision and to build up the wall to protect Jerusalem. Leaders often fail to have faith in the abilities of their associates at work. The same leaders often fail to have faith in the abilities of their family members. Leaders who lack faith in people at work or at home will fail to give ambitious challenges to stretch their abilities and to seek higher goals in life. A vision that is compelling and has people's support provides the strength to accomplish the stretch to achieve higher goals. Nehemiah's vision to make Jerusalem a safe place to live was a stretch goal. His vision rallied the people, and they achieved the goal.

The role of the leader is a difficult one. Vision, knowledge, and communications must come together with energy, enthusiasm, and divine guidance to lead the organization into the future. In addition, the leader must have the physical and mental stamina to pursue the vision, to monitor progress and to stay the course. Regularly scheduled exercise is time well spent to develop this physical and mental confidence. A leader's role is to bring change. Some people will be eager to accept it while others will work to reject the changes. The lesson here is to expect, plan and prepare for the strife change causes. Most people do not like change and subscribe to the old axiom, "if it is not broke, don't fix it." The old ways did not seem broken to many when Jesus came on the scene, but change was necessary. Leaders in power in Christ's time were not able or did not want to see that their corrupt acts violated God's plan. Jesus brought change. He also recognized that change could cause division. Luke expresses this in his gospel.

Luke 12: 51-52
Suppose ye that I am come to give peace on earth? Nay: but rather division: For from henceforth there shall be five in one household divided, three against two, and two against three.

The same is true in the work place. Change can create division among associates so a leader must handle change thoughtfully to minimize conflicts.

Even strong leaders have human fragility and weakness that can lead to discouragement. They must trust their teams, stay the course, and not let discouragement win the day. Luke gives us Jesus' words that we should stay the course and not let doubt, or the comfort of the old ways deter us from moving forward.

Luke 9:62
And Jesus said unto him, No man, having put his hand to the plough, and looking back, is fit for the kingdom of God.

People promoted through the ranks have special change management difficulties. This is especially true of younger workers promoted because they are capable and very mature for their age. They may have to lead people who they worked for, or worked with, along the way. To convince others to accept and trust a peer placed in a leadership position is not an easy thing. It takes patience and communications to build trust. We see things as we expect them to be. People hired from other businesses and consultants have a mysterious wisdom attached to them because we sometimes believe they know more than the people we know. Internal people have well known backgrounds, which includes their strengths, weaknesses, and sometimes, resentments. We tend to give more credibility to the mysterious new people with unknown backgrounds as opposed to people we know and work with every day. Luke gives a lesson and warning from history for someone internally promoted. The people did not accept Jesus as a prophet in His own country. Likewise, people promoted from inside are not always accepted as a new leader. Luke gives hope for the promoted leader who seeks God's help.

Luke 4:24
And he said, Verily I say unto you, No prophet is accepted in his own country. For with God nothing shall be impossible.

Create business plan strategies

The creation of strategies to achieve the vision is another large step on the road to complete the business plan. A written list of strategies is essential to achieve consistent communications across the organization that result in a constancy of purpose. It also allows leaders to down load their thoughts onto paper to free up capacity in their minds for more thoughtful deliberation. Formation of a written strategy is a process that requires the leader to use communications, planning and diplomacy. It is important that the leader call on God's help. Psalms tells us it takes God's help to build a successful career.

> **Psalms 127:1**
> Except the Lord build the house, they labour in vain that build it: except the Lord keep the city, the watchman waketh but in vain.

Many organizations lack agreement on direction and constancy of purpose. The employees do not understand where their business is going in the future and how their work can contribute to overall success. Common complaints are that "No one tells us anything" and "The employees and departments don't work together or share information. They are going in their own direction." A leader breaks down the barriers between people and groups to get them to focus and work together to arrive at consensus on vision, strategies, and related goals. Only a good listener will find the barriers that prevent progress and eliminate them to achieve success. A leader must take the time to listen, absorb, and not judge. Thoughtfully reflecting on input, and especially that which is disagreeable, may open the door to solve issues that are holding back progress. In Proverbs and Colossians, we get a lesson to listen and to respond with respect. The penalty for not listening is the growth of unrest and resentment and the reinforcement of barriers that limit communication and organizational growth.

> **Proverbs 15:1**
> A soft answer turneth away wrath: but grievous words stir up anger.

Colossians 4:6
Let your speech be always with grace, seasoned with salt, that ye may know how ye ought to answer every man.

Strategy development requires a lot of ideas and input just as the vision statement required inputs and ideas. Associates will hold back their ideas if they are judged too quickly and not given a fair evaluation. Ideas, when accepted and appreciated, increase the flow of information. Write down all the ideas during strategy development sessions without judgment and then later combine or eliminate them. This encourages the flow of ideas. Keep copies of all the ideas presented, as they can prove valuable in a future review. A weak idea today many times can be a great idea tomorrow. St. Paul warns us not to be proud and judge others too quickly.

1 Corinthians 4:4-5
For I know nothing by myself; yet am I not hereby justified: but he that judgeth me is the Lord. Therefore, judge nothing before the time, until the Lord come, who both will bring to light the hidden things of darkness, and will make manifest the counsels of the hearts: and then shall every man have praise of God.

Communicate the business plan

Communicating the business plan is a major challenge. There is usually a long period from the start of the planning process to when leadership is ready to communicate the finished plan. The plan includes the business purpose, vision, and strategies. Each of these elements is a difficult job to complete. Many people may have helped to prepare the plan, but not many know the entire plan because they participated in only some of the preparations. A lot of time may have been required to get the draft plan together and memories are sometimes weak. Start the communication process with a review of the purpose and the vision. The purpose statement describes the business you are in and the vision statement describes how you will be successful in that business. Associates must understand and buy into these two elements before they move beyond this point and into strategy development. Proverbs tells us the vision communication is critical to rally the organization, to keep it focused and to keep it energized.

Proverbs 29:18
Where there is no vision, the people perish: but he that keepeth the law, happy is he.

Present the purpose, vision, and strategies in a compelling manner but one that keeps the door open to incorporate new associate ideas. Recognize company history and past accomplishments. This builds support with employees who have labored hard for many years to get the business where it is today. It is important to acknowledge and celebrate these past works and answer concerns during this stage to eliminate negativity. Accomplishments of the past must blend into the plans for the future to produce a cohesive team over all tenures.

Communication plans are necessary to ensure information reaches everyone. Invest time and energy to ensure the plan is comprehensive, and this will build trust, respect, and commitment. Poor communications create confusion. This confusion can delay progress for months while people seek clarifications. James warns us that what we say can be very powerful but also harmful if not thought through. A poorly worded statement can be the spark that causes a great conflagration of mistrust and anger among people.

James 3:5-6
Even so, the tongue is a little member, and boasteth great things. Behold, how great a matter a little fire kindleth! And the tongue is a fire, a world of iniquity: so is the tongue among our members, that it defileth the whole body, and setteth on fire the course of nature; and it is set on fire of hell.

Leaders should not use a secret agenda to achieve a different vision than stated, nor should they manipulate support information to gain agreement. The truth always finds a way to make itself known and when this happens all credibility will be lost. You can never fully recover lost credibility. Luke's gospel warns us that nothing stays hidden for long.

Luke 12:2-3
For there is nothing covered, that shall not be revealed; neither hid, that shall not be known. Therefore, whatsoever ye have spoken in darkness shall be heard in the light; and that which ye have spoken in the ear in closets shall be proclaimed upon the housetops.

Employees need to have a clear picture that their hard work to implement a business plan will benefit them. Plans presented to employees must be simple, rational and the desired outcome must be clear. This is always a difficult picture to paint. Overselling the employees with too many facts or numbers leads to confusion. The basis for the numbers may not be entirely clear and employees who do not have a strong financial or math education may lose sight of the end goal in a forest of numbers. Test the presentation with a small focus group, which represents a cross section of the organization, to help paint a clear picture. Ecclesiastes tells us that we need to be frugal, clear with our words, and not speak as a pompous self-promoting boaster.

Ecclesiastes 5:2-3
Be not rash with thy mouth, and let not thine heart be hasty to utter anything before God: for God is in heaven, and thou upon earth: therefore let thy words be few. For a dream cometh through the multitude of business; and a fool's voice is known by multitude of words.

Clear vision statements segregate the numerical goals that may change annually from the long-term business objectives. A business may have the purpose to be a home maintenance service and may have, for example, a simple vision statement like, "Our business provides home maintenance services that rate a perfect "10" for quality and service and our expert technicians treat customers as family."

State the financial results separately, "Our goal is to increase the share in this $40 million dollar business in North America from the current 10%, $4 million, to 25% or $10 million." This separation of information ensures that the vision statement is easy to remember, and secondly it ensures that even if the financial performance numbers change, the vision will not. It is important to analyze the business environment in North America to ensure the benefits are credible. The benefits must show that the employees' hard work will produce significant financial gain and personal growth worthy of everyone's efforts.

Businesses do not work in a vacuum; competitors may exist that provide similar services. The products and services offered must have a distinct differentiation from what the competition offers to assure a chance to gain customers. The vision statement should emphasize what differentiates the business from other businesses. Analyze competitor performance to be sure there is a distinct difference that will drive success. Pride can be an enemy if we believe we can be successful just because we are better than the competition. Many businesses fail because they have no stronger differentiation in their vision than they are more intelligent or they will work harder than the competition. James tells us it takes wisdom and humility to create a unique business proposition.

James 3:13
Who is a wise man and endued with knowledge among you? Let him shew out of a good conversation his works with meekness of wisdom.

Strategies to grow a business always require something to change. Growth can rattle the nerves of people who feel secure in their current environment, and this is a majority of the people. Do not ignore the inherent insecurity associates may have with change. Take the time to understand them and help them make the change. Luke tells us that change is fundamental to life. The new must replace the old to achieve success. Employees may resist future change even though changes made in the past yielded positive results. Many will say that yesterday's success does not guarantee future success. Luke tells us that we cannot cling to the past. We must overcome prejudices to be able to grow and prosper.

> **Luke 5:36-39**
> And he spake also a parable unto them; No man putteth a piece of a new garment upon an old; if otherwise, then both the new maketh a rent, and the piece that was taken out of the new agreeth not with the old. And no man putteth new wine into old bottles; else, the new wine will burst the bottles, and be spilled, and the bottles shall perish. But new wine must be put into new bottles; and both are preserved. No man also having drunk old wine straightway desireth new: for he saith, the old is better.

Get customers and stakeholders involved

Customers and stakeholders play a critical role in the business plan formation. The vision and strategies need to show the customer a compelling differentiation from the competition. The customers must be able to see the benefits without too much persuasion to convince them. Customers need to feel the strategies will help them achieve their vision and goals and convince them that a long-term partnership will benefit both parties. Corinthians tells us that we must have the same goals and be part of a common plan. The vision and strategies serve to unite the organization's management, employees, and customers to a common cause.

> **1 Corinthians 1:10**
> Now I beseech you, brethren, by the name of our Lord Jesus Christ, that ye all speak the same thing, and that there be no divisions among you; but that ye be perfectly joined together in the same mind and in the same judgment.

Customers want more than agreements. They want follow up progress reports. Leaders must keep commitments, even verbal ones, with customers or stakeholders. They need to report regularly the progress made on performance commitments or changes the customers expect. This builds trust. Ecclesiastes warns us to be true to what we say.

Ecclesiastes 5:5
Better is it that thou shouldest not vow, than that thou shouldest vow and not pay.

Help people accept change

How do you get a four hundred pound gorilla to share his bananas? You don't unless he wants to share them. This is a change management joke. Unless the person wants to make a change, the person will not support the change. There is a lot of truth to this especially when we try to change people's habits in the workplace. They must want to change for the change to be effective.

Negativism is one of the first hurdles to overcome to clear the way for the work ahead. Present the business plan with sufficient background information to convince people that it is achievable. Comments like, "we're already working too hard," "we don't have enough resources," and "the competitors will fight back to defend their turf" are to be expected. Anticipate questions and carefully prepare responses beforehand that will win the day and gain commitment.

Complaints are also cries for help to make things better since most employees realize, but may not admit, that their livelihoods depend on the business's success. People may fear change, but they are even more fearful of losing their job if the business is not competitive. People have complained throughout history with the hope to improve their situation. Job shows us in scripture that people complained in ancient times and even to God. Complaints will always be part of life so it is important that we accept them without bitterness and deal with them fairly.

Job 23:2-6
Even today is my complaint bitter: my stroke is heavier than my groaning. Oh that I knew where I might find him! That I might

come even to his seat! I would order my cause before him, and fill my mouth with arguments. I would know the words, which he would answer me, and understand what he would say unto me. Will he plead against me with his great power? No; but he would put strength in me.

Associate complaints can be pathways to improvement and better customer service. Employees should be open, albeit diplomatic, with their complaints and not let them fester and cause derision. Accept a complaint as a potential idea for improvement and do not take the complaint personally or as an attack on the business plan.

It is important not to be dismissive or too quick to answer complaints. Take every complaint seriously. Delve into complaints from associates to understand the facts behind their remarks. The root cause for the complaint may not be obvious even to the complainant. Researching the problem will make the response more credible. A person may complain that his arm gets tired because of his work. An inattentive listener may pass this over as just an employee who is a chronic complainer. An attentive listener would delve more deeply into the situation and may find that the employee's workstation design is the cause of the pain. This discovery would result in a redesign of the workstation that increases efficiency. When all the workstations use the new design, the company will save significant labor cost. In addition, a second benefit would be a reduction in high medical costs from employees injured using the old workstation design. Understand and probe the cause of a complaint as it can lead to profitable improvement.

It is better for an employee to have the opportunity to discuss issues than hold them in which leads to poor morale. The employee has the obligation to be straightforward and honest. Paul in his letters to the Ephesians and Philippians tells us to remove walls between us, warns against deceptive muttering and complaints, and tells us how to conduct ourselves in truth.

Ephesians 2:14-15, 4:25, 6:6
For he is our peace, who hath made both one, and hath broken down the middle wall of partition between us; Do all things without murmurings and disputing's: That ye may be blameless and harmless, the sons of God, without rebuke, in the midst of a crooked and perverse nation, among whom ye shine as lights in the world; Wherefore putting away lying, speak every man truth with his neighbour: for we are members one of another. Not with eye service, as men pleasers; but as the servants of Christ, doing the will of God from the heart;

A simple law of physics states that a body in motion at a constant speed will stay in motion at the same speed unless an applied force causes it to change speed. This applies to business. Apply a force to speed up business growth; otherwise, the business will cease to grow and eventually decline as negative competitive forces are applied. In the business world, growth is a necessity. Stagnation often leads to decline as competitors pick away at the business, and the high cost to advertise to maintain market share erodes profits. God did not encourage the status quo. As noted in Deuteronomy, He encouraged Moses and his people to move on and change what they were doing. He did not want them to continue to dwell in their current comfort zone. Instead, He wanted them to move on and improve their situation. They had an incentive, the Promised Land, if they took the challenge to go forward. God provides all of us with great opportunities if we allow our minds to be open and follow His direction.

Deuteronomy 1:5-8
On this side Jordan, in the land of Moab, began Moses to declare this law, saying, The Lord our God spake unto us in Horeb, saying, Ye have dwelt long enough in this mount: Turn you, and take your journey, and go to the mount of the Amorites, and unto all the places nigh thereunto, in the plain, in the hills, and in the vale, and in the south, and by the sea side, to the land of the Canaanites, and unto Lebanon, unto the great river, the river Euphrates. Behold, I

have set the land before you: go in and possess the land which the Lord sware unto your fathers, Abraham, Isaac, and Jacob, to give unto them and to their seed after them.

Deuteronomy tells us that God expressed a sense of urgency for the people to move forward. Organizations must have a sense of urgency to get things done so they can outperform the competition. Create faster response times with work process designs that remove non-value added steps that slow people down. It is frustrating for motivated associates when they run into administrative or other barriers that slow their progress. Educate associates why urgency helps the business's competitive position. Urgency appeals to customers because it makes them feel like their needs are your highest priority. This provides a competitive advantage. In Luke's gospel, Jesus expresses this urgency to get things done and not make excuses. He reprimands a follower who makes an excuse not to continue a journey with Him so he can see his family.

Luke 9:61-62
And another also said, Lord, I will follow thee; but let me first go bid them farewell, which are at home at my house. And Jesus said unto him, No man, having put his hand to the plough, and looking back, is fit for the kingdom of God.

Break down communication barriers
Turf protection is a deadly reality in most organizations. Many organizations fail because of silo thinking. Managers who give first priority to protect their turf rather than to help team members cause silo thinking. The silos they create allow them to store and covet information, relationships, or resources in a protected shell so they look better at the expense of the overall organization. People who seek to improve themselves at the expense of others work against God's plan. Proverbs warns us that self-interest profits no one.

Proverbs 10:2
Treasures of wickedness profit nothing: but righteousness delivereth from death.

Managers create silos not only to self-promote, but in some cases, to demote their fellow managers when they withhold information or spread false rumors. This brings great conflict between entities that spells doom for the organization. Mark points out a house divided cannot stand.

Mark 3:25
And if a house be divided against itself, that house cannot stand.

Leadership creates silos when it does not provide adequate communication tools and information links between departments or data systems. One part of the business, whose communications are well designed, may stand out as top notch in a customer's eyes, like order taking, while another part, like shipping, which has a poor communication system may fail to live up to the customer's expectations. The result is lost business.

Proactively address poor communications that result from silo-minded managers who withhold information even when the technology is there to share it. Leaders need to penalize silo managers who hoard information especially when it leads to customer issues. Matthew tells us that a manager must have loyalty to the whole business and not to personal self-interest. He warns us to be selective in the masters we serve. The masters that a leader must avoid are pride, loftiness, and profit for profit's sake. Pride keeps leaders from taking responsibility for mistakes and closes their mind to ideas other than their own. A lofty leader will not find it easy to show people respect, and respect of each individual is important to successful leadership. Profits are important to be able to do good works, but profits for profits sake works against God's plan for us to help others.

Matthew 6:24
No man can serve two masters: for either he will hate the one, and love the other; or else he will hold to the one, and despise the other. Ye cannot serve God and mammon.

Proactive leaders prevent silos when they provide technologies and encouragement to communicate information. They set a good example when they share information freely and when they personally use the technologies they provide. Associates generally conform to the style that leaders demonstrate either by their words or by their actions. Leaders who do not learn to use new technologies to improve their performance will encourage associates to follow their poor example. Leaders can create poor morale if they use updated technologies, like the best cellphones, but let their employees struggle with old and slow equipment. This can strain relations, which harms teamwork. Actions always speak louder than words.

Promote teamwork

One manager who worked for me loved to tell his peers jokingly, "I am a team player; I am just not on your team." Leaders have a challenge to get everyone on the same team.

A leader needs to be sympathetic to everyone's viewpoint. However, an individual cannot roadblock team progress. It is important to recognize and reward teamwork. This creates a positive team culture of shared experiences versus one based on negativity and self-interests. The team must rely on each other to be able to adapt itself quickly to new challenges and the implementation of new methods. Paul reminds us that we need to avoid silo conflicts in the work place and work with each other to build the organization.

> **Galatians 5:15**
> But if ye bite and devour one another, take heed that ye be not consumed one of another.

People with divergent viewpoints must be ready to work as part of the team and be able to compromise with their teammates when appropriate to help the whole team move forward. People who cannot work with a team must be removed and assigned work that is more singular in nature least they destroy the team. When people work together, their collective knowledge grows exponentially through the interaction of their thoughts. One thought shared by a person can generate several additional thoughts by other team members. Proverbs emphasizes the point that one person can energize another.

> **Proverbs 27:17**
> Iron sharpeneth iron; so a man sharpeneth the countenance of his friend.

Teams also provide support to the business to help fight off aggressive competitors. Sports teams set a good example for business. Team members that work well together know they cannot monopolize the ball in play for their own glory. They need to share it and the glory to achieve victory. There is always a negative pushback from team members and from the fans when one player tries to monopolize the play. Ecclesiastes provides essential instruction about the support people get when they work together.

> **Ecclesiastes 4:9-12**
> Two are better than one; because they have a good reward for their labour. For if they fall, the one will lift up his fellow: but woe to him that is alone when he falleth; for he hath not another to help him up. Again, if two lie together, then they have heat: but how can one be warm alone? And if one prevails against him, two shall withstand him; and a threefold cord is not quickly broken.

Sell the strategy to all levels

There is no contributor too big or too small who cannot be an asset to help implement a business plan. A written communication plan ensures that associates who are part of the implementation team get the information they need to be effective. It takes time, energy, and patience to ensure that there is alignment and cooperation to move ahead. Everyone must have the opportunity to provide input into the plan, and to ask questions. This achieves consistency of purpose. Holding large meetings to get commitment is not new. Joshua shows us how a leader got his people together to gain their commitment. He invites them to depart the house he heads if they cannot be part of the team and commit themselves to help make the plan work. This is an important point since the followers have a responsibility to support the organization even if they do not fully agree with the direction.

> **Joshua 24:1, 15**
> And Joshua gathered all the tribes of Israel to Shechem, and called for the elders of Israel, and for their heads, and for their judges, and for their officers; and they presented themselves before God. And if it seems evil unto you to serve the Lord, choose you this day whom ye will serve; whether the gods, which your fathers served that, were on the other side of the flood, or the gods of the Amorites, in whose land ye dwell: but as for me and my house, we will serve the Lord.

The business we are not in

A vision statement helps the employees to see what the business is about and where it is going. Just as importantly, these same employees must also understand what the business does not want to do. It is critical to explain what "is not" the business to keep the focus on "what is" the business. Avoid placing associates into low value endeavors that are not fundamental to achieve the vision. If home maintenance is the intended focus, do we want to do room additions? Examples of what is not the business should be supported by information that explains why these are not reasonable profitable paths to pursue. Logical extensions to the products and services offered may not be possible to pursue now because of a lack of resources. Resource availability is often the main reason the business must focus on only a few things at first. However, associates need to keep their eyes and ears open to new ideas from customers that they can implement in the future when resources are available. Future profits may allow the scope of the business to expand and use the new ideas. Nevertheless, it is best to make progress in achievable bites, supported with sufficient resources, while we keep an eye on the long-term target.

Develop performance parameters

Strategies require a clear set of performance parameters to monitor progress. The parameters will be the milestones against which the employees measure their performance. Parameters that align the overall strategy with each employee's work make each employee more accountable. Typical parameters might be market share, market penetration, per unit production cost, and customer complaints. Parameter selection requires a thoughtful review to determine the key things that will drive success. They may be both internal and customer focused priorities. Using an outside resource to lead the staff through the selection of parameters can provide an unbiased analysis. The outside source can also provide the basic research data to help select the best performance factors for the staff to monitor. Staff members frequently do not have the time, resources, or skill to assemble this type of information. Money spent to support the staff through this part of the strategy development process will be a clear sign that the work is serious and that support will be there for them now and in the future. Corinthians offers good advice when it tells us a leader must invest in the business and give the employees the resources they need with a cheerful face.

> **2 Corinthians 9:6-7**
> But this I say, He which soweth sparingly shall reap also sparingly; and he which soweth bountifully shall reap also bountifully. Everyman according as he purposeth in his heart, so let him give; not grudgingly, or of necessity: for God loveth a cheerful giver.

The research into, and compilation of, performance parameters usually shows that there are many things to accomplish to make the business a success. These may be to reduce costs to attract more customers, improve quality or service levels, offer new products or services, offer specific training, or improve customer communications. However, several critical elements usually head the list and each will have a priority against which we allocate resources. Four to six elements generally form the strategic plan under which we can group many other tasks. These key elements form the strategic pillars that support the business plan and vision. Each pillar contains several things to accomplish to meet that individual pillar's objectives. For instance, quality may be one strategic pillar. Individual building blocks to support this pillar would be to reduce customer complaints, reduce production defects, improve supplier quality, and train employees. Each of these would have a goal for improvement during the year that would help the business to achieve its vision. Success with one pillar is important, but it is just one of several strong pillars needed to keep the business plan from collapsing.

Set aggressive goals

Once the "what" and "how to" of the business plan strategy is completed, challenge the group to set aggressive goals and timetables. This includes both long and short-term goals. A leader's cheerful commitment to provide resources to achieve these goals builds the associates' confidence. Teams should feel the goals are achievable in the timeframe given, even though the goals may require a stretch in performance. It is the leader's responsibility to help make everyone a success and ensure that enthusiastic associates do not over extend themselves and get in trouble. Associates need to support the leader with thoughtful input and hard work since their futures are at stake. Leaders in their personal interactions return the trust and commitment given when they provide support and accessibility to solve problems. Matthew's words suggest the interaction required between team members at all levels.

> **Matthew 7:12**
> Therefore all things whatsoever ye would that men should do to you, do ye even so to them: for this is the law and the prophets.

Customer and Market Focus

Nothing is new in the world
In the lobby of our offices were several display boards of products, both our competitors, and ours sold since the early 1900's. It was interesting to see how many of these products were reformatted and reintroduced successfully to the market over time. It takes more than a unique product to be successful in the market. It takes collaboration with employees and customers to sell in a new product line or service.

> **Ecclesiastes 1:9**
> The thing that hath been, it is that which shall be; and that which is done is that which shall be done: and there is no new thing under the sun.

Respect your stakeholders
Ecclesiastes points out that there is nothing new under the sun. Few people have original ideas or unique knowledge about a topic. Customers are smart people who have experienced and seen many things. Leaders must accept that they are dealing with intuitive and experienced people, and leaders should give customers the respect they deserve. A leader motivated by greed and who bends the truth is doomed to fail. Experienced customers can see through these tricks and then all trust is lost. The focus should be to build a sincere long-term mutually beneficial partnership. Ecclesiastes notes that the key to success is to establish a name that customers respect.

> **Ecclesiastes 7:1**
> A good name is better than precious ointment; and the day of death than the day of one's birth.

Do not judge people by their outward appearance. We can be deceived when it comes to their ability to afford services or their level of intelligence. Many times people who can most afford to make purchases do not show outward signs of wealth. Treat all who seek services with equal respect but at the same time with good business caution. James tells us that outward appearance can fool us. We should treat all people with the same respect.

James 2:2-4
For if there come unto your assembly a man with a gold ring, in goodly apparel, and there come in also a poor man in vile raiment; And ye have respect to him that weareth the gay clothing, and say unto him, Sit thou here in a good place; and say to the poor, Stand thou there, or sit here under my footstool: Are ye not then partial in yourselves, and are become judges of evil thoughts?

Good business practice dictates that we trust only what can be verified. "Don't you trust me" is not a statement a mature businessperson should use in a conversation. Both parties should understand that it is not a matter of trust between people; it is just good business practice to verify facts. Business stakeholders include associates, customers, and stockholders. They want their business investment protected from backroom deals and unscrupulous acts. Verbal agreements verified in a court of law have legal status. Written agreements are easier to enforce. The process to write out an agreement gives everyone time to think and not overlook important details. Sincere people do not mind written agreements especially when the agreements make the business terms clearer for both parties. Written statements enhance communications and preserve trust by minimizing misunderstandings.

Be direct and honest with customers

No foolproof approach is available to win over a customer or a market area. Start with research to determine how to position the business in the market so there is a distinct differentiation with the competition. If the competitor has a high priced low volume premium product, a low cost basic product that gains higher volume may provide the right differentiation. Describe to the customer the attributes of the services and products offered in direct and honest terms. A message delivered based on innuendo or snappy advertisements will leave the consumer confused about the real benefits.

Television commercials entertain us, but afterward we often realize we did not understand the message of the commercial or even remember the name of the advertiser. The message must be clear and easy to understand. Matthew gives sound advice to show product or service benefits in the open light of day. We should avoid messages that are like the bushel in the scripture that hides the benefit.

Matthew 5:15
Neither do men light a candle, and put it under a bushel, but on a candlestick; and it giveth light unto all that are in the house.

Put yourself in their shoes
Effective leaders have the ability to put themselves in the shoes of their associates or customers to see things from their perspective. This concept seems easy to grasp, but it is not always easy to do. By their nature, leaders are gregarious and demonstrative in their actions. They are usually visionaries. These attributes seem counter to the associates' and customers' need to have the leader patiently listen, understand their situation, and help them to accomplish their vision and goals. The customer's business plan may not align with a strategy the business leader has in regard to a specific customer group. A customer's direction may even appear to slow or restrict growth plans or a customer may appear at first glance to be unknowingly going down a disastrous path. It would be presumptuous to think the customer is wrong and suggest a change. Credibility is established when the facts are checked before recommendations are made. The leader must have the endurance and patience to see the discussions through before making suggestions. Gathering the facts before jumping in with ideas also lends credibility to future recommendations. Proverbs reminds us that loose comments can lead to disaster but fact-finding research and perseverance pays off.

Proverbs 10:4
He becometh poor that dealeth with a slack hand: but the hand of the diligent maketh rich.

To keep profitable customers, the leader must walk in their shoes and adjust strategies to create a "win-win" situation. St. Paul reminds us to move forward purposefully and with grace when we try to deliver a message to associates or customers.

Colossians 4:5-6
Walk in wisdom toward them that are without, redeeming the time. Let your speech be always with grace, seasoned with salt, that ye may know how ye ought to answer every man.

Businesses that survive the test of time offer goods or services that make customers want to come back. Advertisement works to get customers to try a product or service, but no amount of advertisement will keep customers if they are ultimately unhappy with what they buy. Most long-term customers will overlook a short-term product or service failure and stay with a supplier. However, customers will quickly switch allegiance if an unfavorable trend develops. The competition will work to emphasize these shortcomings in an attempt to attract the customers. This is very evident in the political arena where competitors can be ruthless in their efforts to dethrone a rival by emphasizing the opponent's real or perceived shortcomings. This type of rivalry is similar in the business world but not as personally ruthless. Proverbs warns us to avoid deceitful action against competition because in the end God will destroy the deceitful.

Proverbs 11:3
The integrity of the upright shall guide them: but the perverseness of transgressors shall destroy them.

Customers want a consistent performance from their suppliers and are usually quick to call a supplier and complain when there is a problem. Customers request this type of meeting to emphasize the seriousness of the issue even though they do not intend to discontinue purchases. This is especially true if there is a distinct benefit offered versus the competition. Prepare for the complaint meeting by anticipating questions. Prepare rational responses to reassure the customer that your staff analyzed the problem, a solution is available, and the problem will not reoccur. However, be honest if a solution is not yet available. The ability to take a customer's complaint and still be positive is necessary for a successful relationship. Like a football star, you have to be able to take a hit and still keep a positive outlook to win the game. Ecclesiastes tell us that it is a wise person who solicits, listens, and then reacts to a complaint, versus a person who tries to paint over issues to present a rosy picture.

> **Ecclesiastes 7:5**
> It is better to hear the rebuke of the wise, than for a man to hear the song of fools.

Deepen your customer understanding

Customers understand proposals better when the proposals are in their own business language. Consequently, leaders must get to know their language. Organizations have unique languages that have terms that only they understand. A business' language may use special words to describe departments, programs, products, or employee titles. Look for opportunities to interview multiple staff members across the business to get a better grasp on the big picture and to understand the unique language terms they use. Different parts of the business may not communicate well between themselves but will talk more freely with an independent outsider. The discussions will give a broader information base from which to make suggestions to make your primary contact successful, and become an ally for life. Psalms reminds us that good business people lend well. They lend knowledge, ideas, and even favorable financial terms to help customers. At the same time, diplomacy and discretion are important to avoid creating enemies within the customer's organization.

> **Psalms 112:5**
> A good man sheweth favour, and lendeth: he will guide his affairs with discretion.

Customers are always right even when they are wrong. Meetings are not a stage to complain or argue about the ills of the customer's programs or the industry. Meetings are a time to probe, gather, and glean information to form the basis of strategies and goals. These customer meetings may even cause the vision or strategy to change to take advantage of a need in the market. Proverbs encourages us to seek what is good for customers, and we will benefit.

Proverbs 11:27
He that diligently seeketh good procureth favour: but he that seeketh mischief, it shall come unto him.

Profits enable good works

Businesses must make profits to support their employees and meet their social obligations to the community. Business, therefore, must have a plan that will make a profit or achieve a charitable objective in the case of a non-profit organization. Profits are a good thing as they make good works possible, and making money is an indicator that your work provides a needed service that benefits others. Not being profitable is a sign of failure even though there may be many uncontrollable variables that can cause us to miss a profit target. Leaders who find they are making more excuses than profits need to admit their shortcomings and seek outside help. St. Paul tells us that workers who labor hard should expect to reap the benefits of the harvest.

1 Corinthians 9:10
Or saith he it altogether for our sakes? For our sakes, no doubt, this is written: that he that ploweth should plow in hope; and that he that thresheth in hope should be partaker of his hope.

Nothing stands still in the business world. Stay alert to changing world trends in order to develop a plan that has the versatility to survive over time. An effective plan for products and services requires the strategic placement of efforts into areas that will produce the best returns over the longest time possible to reward the efforts expended. To develop a market is expensive and time consuming, and there needs to be sufficient return over the life of the product or service to justify the investment. Nothing lasts forever. A leader must seek new opportunities to replace the existing ones that are on decline. It is a big competitive world and there are always places into which a business can venture and be successful. Businesses exist in an ever-changing environment of companies that move up in the world and companies that fail. New technologies kill off old industries and start new ones. Shifts in customers' preferences and demographics require new products to replace old ones. The next great profitable business enterprise is always on the horizon. This will continue to be ad infinitum. Do not assume today's profits will continue long into the future. Ecclesiastes reminds us that all things including businesses are temporary and have their season.

Ecclesiastes 3:1
To everything, there is a season, and a time to every purpose under the heaven:

Generate new life

A leader must have a strategy to generate new life in the organization. This applies to improving staff capabilities, product upgrades, and new products. Luke tells us that salt, like business products and services, can lose its freshness and become worthless with time. A leader cannot replace the old salt with new salt without a plan to carry the new product to a higher level to maintain profits into the future.

Luke 14:34
Salt is good: but if the salt have lost his savour, wherewith shall it be seasoned?

Products and services placed in the right market quadrant for price, volume and service level relative to the competition will win, but their position must also have safeguards. Without a competitive barrier to entry, a new venture may become engaged in a price war from the day of introduction causing margins and profits to disappear. Barriers to entry can be long-term contracts, patents, unique technologies or service delivery methodologies that a competitor cannot easily replicate overnight. The right barrier puts the competitor in a difficult position. Competitors who want to remove the barriers may need to make investments, which they cannot afford to make, or require them to abandon an expensive technology or process and start in a new unfamiliar direction. Barriers protect your business from aggressors who want to take advantage of your success. In Exodus, we hear how a barrier protected the Israelites from the pursuing Egyptian army. This story serves as a reminder to us of the importance of barriers to business survival.

> **Exodus 14:19-23, 26**
> And the angel of God, which went before the camp of Israel, removed and went behind them; and the pillar of the cloud went from before their face, and stood behind them: And it came between the camp of the Egyptians and the camp of Israel; and it was a cloud and darkness to them, but it gave light by night to these: so that the one came not near the other all the night. And Moses stretched out his hand over the sea; and the Lord caused the sea to go back by a strong east wind all that night, and made the sea dry land, and the waters were divided. And the children of Israel went into the midst of the sea upon the dry ground: and the waters were a wall unto them on their right hand, and on their left. And the Egyptians pursued, and went in after them to the midst of the sea, even all Pharaoh's horses, his chariots, and his horsemen. And the Lord said unto Moses, Stretch out thine hand over the sea, that the waters may come again upon the Egyptians, upon their chariots, and upon their horsemen.

Be persistent

Making a sale is as much an art as a science. There are many skills required to complete a sale. These include customer marketing assistance, financial benefits analysis, and negotiation of contracts. Nothing ever happens overnight so be prepared for a long struggle. Luke reminds us that perseverance pays off.

Luke 18:1-5
And he spake a parable unto them to this end, that men ought always to pray, and not to faint; Saying, There was in a city a judge, which feared not God, neither regarded man: And there was a widow in that city; and she came unto him, saying, Avenge me of mine adversary. And he would not for a while: but afterward he said within himself, Though I fear not God, nor regard man; Yet because this widow troubleth me, I will avenge her, lest by her continual coming she weary me.

Customers are so busy that the first inclination when approached with a proposal is to say no, just to minimize their stress level. They do not want to think about one more thing. Being a nag is not an effective perseverance plan, as this just increases the tension and stress. To be effective, a perseverance plan must include a list of things that will benefit the customer's business and reduce the customer's personal stress level. A business lunch or free seminar is a great way to get customers out of their stressful work environment and into a place with fewer distractions, where they can focus on your proposals. Luke also reminds us to ask God for help and doors will open.

Luke 11:5-10
And he said unto them, Which of you shall have a friend, and shall go unto him at midnight, and say unto him, Friend, lend me three loaves; For a friend of mine in his journey is come to me, and I have nothing to set before him? And he from within shall answer and say, Trouble me not: the door is now shut, and my children are with me in bed; I cannot rise and give thee. I say unto you, Though he will not rise and give him, because he is his friend, yet because of his importunity he will rise and give him as many as

he needeth. And I say unto you, Ask, and it shall be given you; seek, and Ye shall find; Knock, and it shall be opened unto you. For every one that asketh receiveth; and he that seeketh findeth; and to him that knocketh it shall be opened.

Delegate responsibility

Delegation is not just a method to parcel out work to get things done. It also has the purpose to get more eyes and ears involved in the business. Front line workers receive product and service performance feedback well before top management as the workers are closer to the action and see results first hand. Leadership may hear of issues much later because of reporting time lags. Feedback filtered through multiple levels distorts the message. Each level edits the message a little more. By the time it reaches the decision maker, the problem may not appear to be a serious issue. This long communications link means that it is incumbent on the leader to push decision responsibility down to the people who have first hand, unfiltered knowledge of events. This enables most problems and situations to be resolved before they have time to grow into significant issues.

Deuteronomy tells us how Moses could not carry the burden of leadership by himself, so he delegated responsibility down to the lowest level. In doing so, he created a structured organization of responsible leaders.

Deuteronomy 1:12-15

How can I myself alone bear your cumbrance, and your burden, and your strife? Take you wise men, and understanding, and known among your tribes, and I will make them rulers over you. And ye answered me, and said, The thing which thou hast spoken is good for us to do. So I took the chief of your tribes, wise men, and known, and made them heads over you, captains over thousands, and captains over hundreds, and captains over fifties, and captains over tens, and officers among your tribes.

Customers do not like to wait for answers while their issues move slowly up the corporate chain for resolution. They want to deal with decision makers who can keep things moving in this fast-paced world. Give front line decision makers the authority to spend money and quickly solve problems. Some companies allow employees to spend one thousand dollars or more to solve a problem before they must get approval from their supervisor. The money spent might be a credit to a customers' account for a damaged item received or for a free replacement item sent to the customer. The loss of a customer is far more financially disastrous than if an employee spends a few dollars to keep a customer happy.

Knowledge Management

As we hear from Luke, the effort to collect and make information available to decision makers is not new. It has always been a difficult task, especially before electronic communications. In Caesar's time, it was required to travel to the city of your birth to record the data requested, unlike today when we send in a form via mail or email. Luke's story reminds us that data collection is not an easy task, and it may place a large burden on associates.

> ### Luke 2:1-3
> And it came to pass in those days, that there went out a decree from Caesar Augustus, that all the world should be taxed. (And this taxing was first made when Cyrenius was governor of Syria.) And all went to be taxed, every one into his own city.

Measure and analyze performance

Precise and accurate measurements are important. The business plan achievement requires measurements that monitor progress. In the Bible, there are examples of the measurement precision God required to complete His plans for this world. Exodus reveals to us the precise measurements God dictated to Moses to build the Arc of the Covenant. God required precision in what He wanted built. It was a high priority. This level of precision is required in the business world.

> ### Exodus 27:1
> And thou shalt make an altar of shittim wood, five cubits long, and five cubits broad; the altar shall be foursquare: and the height thereof shall be three cubits.

In the business world, change is inevitable. Plans are best guesses that we modify as we move forward. Vacation driving trips often require an occasional detour or weather related change to the original schedule. Likewise, a business must be flexible, but still keep an eye on the end game.

The time to implement changes or revise strategies can be best determined through periodic measurement and trend analysis. The trends will tell you when to plan a celebration or make a correction.

Leaders want to answer questions like when is the right time to launch a new product, replace worn out equipment or add staff or equipment to handle additional work. Progress reports and sales forecasts give leaders the data to make these decisions. By combining historical data with forecast sales expectations and then extrapolating trends into the future, we are able to predict the important decision dates. Predictions are a guess, but they are vital to ensure resources are available when needed. The lead-time between placing an order and item receipt may be months or years. This is especially true for equipment and production facilities. Suppliers may have several months or years of backlogged work. Failure to get into their schedule early may delay receipt of critical items, inhibit growth, and reduce future profits. A common strategy is to buy a time slot in the supplier's schedule based on the need determined from the extrapolated trend data. This is especially important if the sales of a product or service is growing rapidly and the forecast for future requirements is aggressive. Suppliers receive a penalty payment if the time slot in their schedule is not used. A second strategy is to purchase long lead-time components that have a small value compared to the entire end object. Examples would be a machine component from a busy supplier or a land purchase for a future building. Assess the need to employ these strategies against the potential profit lost if the forecast is correct and customers do not receive their orders.

Customers and employees judge a leader's performance by what the leader communicates to them. Most of all, they look for honesty and they want decisive action when schedules need adjustment. When customers get inaccurate delivery schedules, they can have a disaster because of the obligations they have made to their customers. Do not deceive customers with unrealistic expectations or information that misleads them. Proverbs reminds us that honesty is at the heart of a successful enterprise.

Proverbs 11:1

A false balance is abomination to the Lord: but a just weight is his delight.

Develop a business review calendar

Schedule progress review dates twelve months in advance. Adherence to a review calendar is a critical key performance indicator (KPI), an important milestone measurement of progress toward a goal. Keeping track of meetings scheduled versus meetings held ensures there is a discipline to review progress and not allow performance to slip. Do not review all data at every meeting. The update period may extend out to weekly, monthly, and yearly depending on the data's importance. Daily reviews may be as simple as a fifteen-minute shift change meeting to ensure a smooth shift transition. Question each KPI's usefulness to ensure it is truly meaningful to success. Many feel KPI changes should be made at the end of the year to avoid confusion. You should make midyear changes to key performance indicators if the changes are necessary for year-end success. Do not beat a dead horse to death reviewing useless information!

Proverbs reminds us to keep an eye on the goal and monitor the progress we make on the journey.

Proverbs 4:25-27

Let thine eyes look right on, and let thine eyelids look straight before thee. Ponder the path of thy feet, and let all thy ways be established. Turn not to the right hand nor to the left: remove thy foot from evil.

Business meetings can be the greatest time waster in American industry. They can be productive if an agenda is available before the meeting so everyone is prepared, the meeting has a time limit, and everyone arrives on time. The leader must enforce the discipline to make these things happen. Each person should have a voice at the meeting. The meeting organizer has to control the conversation so the overzealous are controlled and the passive attendees are encouraged to contribute. Everyone invited to a meeting has value to offer. "Still waters run deep," so call on everyone to contribute, even the quiet ones. Your meeting leadership responsibility is not complete until the meeting minutes with agreed follow up actions, responsibilities and completion times are distributed. Meeting minutes are important to summarize results, to place responsibility on people to accomplish specific actions, and to act as an agenda review item for the follow-up meeting. An investment to train meeting facilitators to conduct efficient meetings will have a quick payback and reduce frustration from unproductive meetings.

Data reporting is expensive

Report generation consumes time and money. A person who requests a special report should demonstrate a payback for the costs to generate the report. Train report users to understand the costs to generate reports and they may be more selective in their requests. Most data users do not understand the difficulty to produce reports and are prone to ask for more than they really need. Some computer systems allow users to create their own reports from a database. However, this can cause people to lose focus on their primary job responsibility when they spend too much time on the creation of reports. A careful evaluation of each new report benefits everyone. It is common for a user to have second thoughts about the data or report format needed after a few days of reflection. It is best to do a manual test sample of the data collection and analysis before the resources are committed to make the report permanent. A small investment of time up front to ensure that the final product is useful to the user is time profitably spent. The old adage of "garbage in gets garbage out" is a valid concern. Proverbs tells us not to rush to a conclusion about what we need to do before we hear and understand different inputs. We need to take the time to understand what we need and justify a request we make.

> **Proverbs 18:13**
> He that answereth a matter before he heareth it, it is folly and shame unto him.

Real time data is best

Data collected and used in real time gives the best results. Today's computers and communication technologies allow for more real time data collection and accessibility to the data. Businesses use UPC product scanners at checkout counters and satellite communication to link stores directly to replenishment warehouses. Gas station companies adjust pump prices via satellite to reflect current refinery cost and to maintain a competitive position. However, leaders must use data with care. It is easy to be too involved in data analysis and lose sight of the big picture. Matthew tells us that human perception can be weak. We need to look at the entire forest and not just the individual trees.

> **Matthew 13:14**
> And in them is fulfilled the prophecy of Esaias, which saith, By hearing ye shall hear, and shall not understand; and seeing ye shall see, and shall not perceive:

Design effective information systems

Well-designed information systems give the front line workers the up to date information they need to answer questions and resolve problems on the spot. Customers put on hold become easily frustrated while someone searches for information to solve a problem. To keep customers happy, measure their problem resolution satisfaction and the time it takes to resolve their problem. This includes both customer satisfaction with the assistance given and the employee's satisfaction with the information and resources available to answer the issue. Many companies are proactive in this regard. They ask consumers to take a satisfaction survey after a major purchase, or they tell customers that they are recording their conversation for training purposes. Quality conscience providers frequently use these feedback mechanisms to measure their performance. Ecclesiastes tells us that we cannot predict the future with any certainty. However, we can prepare for it with well-designed information systems.

Ecclesiastes 8:6-7
Because to every purpose there is time and judgment, therefore the misery of man is great upon him. For he knoweth not that which shall be: for who can tell him when it shall be?

Customers and employees must agree that key performance indicators (KPI's) selected to judge their performance are important measures to total business success, even though their contribution may be a small part of the total. Most importantly, employees must feel they have the right tools to achieve high marks for their performance. Leaders know that every person is important, can contribute and add value, even in a small way. Leaders also realize that the sum total of all these small contributions can make or break a business. Many businesses survive on profit margins of just a few percentage points, and the many small contributions provide this margin of profit. Information systems must allow both large and small contributors to participate and build the business. Matthew tells us that the Creator of the world was concerned about the smallest details and that no one was unimportant in the world.

Matthew 10:29-31
Are not two sparrows sold for a farthing? And one of them shall not fall on the ground without your Father. But the very hairs of your head are all numbered. Fear ye not therefore, ye are of more value than many sparrows.

Ensure performance data is reliable

Information reliability is important and most people accept that computer data is accurate. However, associates make mistakes when they collect information and then assemble it into a report. Data that is incorrectly included, excluded or calculated will make the resultant report useless. Decisions made with erroneous data can damage customer relations and business progress. Accurate data is essential to establish trust. Achieve trust with an audit trail of the data from creation to the final report. This task is often not done because it is time consuming, and at times, thankless work. The failure to invest the time to verify data, may result in associates making costly errors, prevent them from solving problems, and cause them to lose customer confidence. Document audit tracks for each piece of data collected using standard techniques as the report is developed. The documentation must be easy to follow so that anyone can check the audit trail. Unfortunately, most report developers do not use standard documentation procedures because it takes time to do this. They are often under pressure to get a new report out so they bypass the documentation step. Failure to document properly has consequences. Report developers may have to redo totally a report that needs a minor change if they cannot understand the data flow. It can take more time to track the data than rewrite the report.

Proverbs reminds us to ensure the truth of the data we use and it will keep us in business for a long time, but data that misrepresents facts causes a short business lifespan.

<u>Proverbs 12:19</u>
The lip of truth shall be established forever: but a lying tongue is but for a moment.

Collect data frugally

Employees use their time most profitably when they spend it with their customers selling goods and services. Collecting too much data can cause a huge distraction to this productive time when associates fill out forms or record unnecessary information for a database. Time is money, and time lost is money lost. Fortunately, modern data processing tools such as product bar code scanning and hand held recording devices make data collection much more efficient. However, leadership can be lulled into thinking that these modern devices solve all the problems of data collection and not appreciate the lost opportunity cost when employees are distracted from their work to collect data. We need to scrutinize carefully the reason to collect data to ensure there are valid and profitable reasons for it. There has always been, and probably will always be a feeling, that historical data is good because "we might be able to use it." Data collected regularly should be the pearls of information that determine the wealth of the organization; otherwise, do not collect it.

Opportunities that require data collection for a short-term study to determine their feasibility should have a cutoff date assigned for the data collection before the project starts. Allocate additional resources to collect the data not to overburden the staff. These resources emphasize the importance management places on people's time to do their normal value added tasks. When the study ends, the data collection should end, which is not always the case. Data collection once initiated has a way of lingering forever as old things stored in a garage. Ecclesiastes reminds us that there is a time to stop unnecessary tasks and throw away things we do not need!

Ecclesiastes 3:6
A time to get, and a time to lose; a time to keep, and a time to cast away;

The time spent to review data can be a burden onto itself. The thought of having to review millions of tiny black numbers printed on reams of paper is enough to make anyone take the day off in despair. Data essentially is dead information that we must resurrect and bring to life to make it meaningful and useful. Habakkuk, in the Old Testament, tells us that the information we provide should inspire the receiver to run with it.

Habakkuk 2:2
And the Lord answered me, and said, Write the vision, and make it plain upon tables, that he may run that readeth it.

Ecclesiastes gives us a lesson about having too much that we can also apply to data systems. It notes that having the right amount is good, but too much increases the number of people, equipment, and cost required to maintain it without an increased benefit to the owner.

Ecclesiastes 5:11
When goods increase, they are increased that eat them: and what good is there to the owners thereof, saving the beholding of them with their eyes?

The right balance of information is difficult to achieve. It requires a survey of employee information needs to help them better interact with customers. Types of data typically requested are customer purchase preferences, previous sales notes, order history, and fulfillment status.

Minimize historical data storage

Data storage is not free. Maintenance of historical data is part of knowledge management. It is often necessary to go back in time and reconstruct a set of events to solve a current problem or understand where a program started to go astray so we can get it back on track. Trend analysis that uses historical data can also be a vibrant tool to monitor progress on decisions made and programs put into place. Government agencies require the retention of data for several years that relates to financial, safety and product quality matters. Good business practice dictates the outside storage of back up information to ensure continuity of the business in the event of a disaster. All these things add to data storage costs. Few people take the time to understand this because they believe it is a small cost not worthy of their attention. We should understand the reasons to retain data, and manage data retention, with review policies that place a cost on data retention. Fortunately, modern computer systems can store more than ever at low cost. This will only get better in the future. However, this should not be a reason to keep all old data.

Ecclesiastes reminds us that laziness and lack of attention to the work we do can lead to poor results. We can control data mismanagement if we expend the energy to keep only useful information whether it is stored in a computer, a file cabinet or on top of a desk.

Ecclesiastes 10:18
By much slothfulness the building decayeth; and through idleness of the hands, the house droppeth through.

Bring information to life
Performance information reports must be full of life to create interest in the employees and customers who review them. The numbers must generate excitement as the scores at a sports stadium excite and rally the fans. This is not to say that we should gloss over bad results or twist information to look good or that delivering bad information should have a funeral feel to it. Information should stress, even with bad results, what we learned from the analysis. Business has spent resources and time over the report period. A positive return on the investment is possible, even with bad results, when we understand what we learned and apply it to improve future performance. Employees and customers react well to visible displays of information like graphs and charts since these can tell a story numbers alone cannot. Fortunately, modern computer software helps to make these presentations easy, but this also requires a trained staff to use these tools. Proverbs gives us a lesson in how not to present information. Information must speak for itself and not be presented in a biased way to bully people toward a selfish viewpoint. Proverbs reminds us that being deceitful, overbearing, or disrespectful will not get the results needed.

Proverbs 6:12-13
A naughty person, a wicked man, walketh with a forward mouth. He winketh with his eyes, he speaketh with his feet, he teacheth with his finger.

Train associates to use data effectively
Associates may not understand what data they should monitor dependent upon their skill and knowledge of the job. Both management and the employees must agree on the data to be reviewed regularly and prioritize the most important factors, that if improved, will move the business forward. These discussions will range throughout the organization since

regional, legal, and even cultural differences in each part of the globe may demand different data solutions. Training is valuable because employees many times find the information and data they need already exists, but they were not aware of it. Confirm with the employees that they have the right data to be successful, and this will relieve stress in their job.

Employees will sometimes disregard the analysis of data and rely more on their intuition or historical knowledge. This can come from a lack of trust of the data, laziness, or lack of analytical abilities. Airplane pilots train to trust the data from their instrumentation more so than their eyes when they are flying through the clouds. Employees who trust and use the data provided will not spend unprofitable time to gather their own data. My factory supervisors to my surprise spent considerable time collecting data and preparing their own employee performance tracking reports. This work kept them in their office and distracted from their main responsibility to be on the production floor helping the employees. It took a considerable amount of effort and coordination with accounting to give the supervisors the information they needed so we could wean them from keeping their own books. Employees need a data problem feedback and resolution process to maintain trust. Information we can trust makes us more confident to use it, improves morale, and makes us productive.

Create positive feedback

Ballparks are a good example of positive data management. Even with bad results, there is always beer and hot dogs consumed in a festive atmosphere. Accompany the communication of results with celebration and positive encouragement of the efforts expended in pursuit of the vision, strategy, and goals. Leaders should recap and refocus the attendees on these elements when appropriate. Do not hold a review meeting without some physical sign of appreciation such as cookies and coffee for employees or a modest lunch for a customer. Employees appreciate physical gifts as a sign of management's gratitude for their efforts. Workers who help to achieve prosperity for the organization should also share in the financial rewards. Ecclesiastes tells us that food and drink are welcome rewards, but money carries the day.

Ecclesiastes 10:19
A feast is made for laughter, and wine maketh merry: but money answereth all things.

Many influences can affect performance. Business results are not always under the control of the employees or customers. External market forces can dramatically affect business both positively and negatively. During difficult times, employees and customers may work harder than ever to achieve only minimal improvement. The business plan may have design defects, which may also negatively affect results despite the effort expended to achieve them. Leaders must have the fortitude to face negative times and keep a positive attitude. Leaders have to reassure associates in difficult times that the game is not over and they can still win despite setbacks. Associates look to their leaders to rally and reassure them. No one else can do it.

Information should correct not criticize

There are good and bad uses of performance data. The purpose to collect, disseminate and review data is to help improve the organization. However, data collection may make employees and customers suspicious of the reasons the data is collected. They may fear we will use the data to punish them rather than to help them. Leaders must be sensitive to this credibility issue. It is counterproductive to credible data use when leaders get angry and criticize associates openly in review meetings, or if they present information in a way that embarrasses associates. Leaders must counsel employees without anger and with respect. They must train managers and supervisors to ensure the proper use and communication of data to both employees and customers. Matthew warns us not to be critical of our brother because it is against God's will.

Matthew 5:22
But I say unto you, That whosoever is angry with his brother without a cause shall be in danger of the judgment: and whosoever shall say to his brother, Raca, shall be in danger of the council: but whosoever shall say, Thou fool, shall be in danger of hell fire.

Focus on being critical of data and not people. Managers who get agreement from employees and customers on performance criteria and measurements have an easier time with employee reviews. Employee bonuses and customer rebates are often dependent on achieving performance standards, and this makes up front agreement on standards critical to avoid conflicts. Paul tells us to chastise people who do not meet expectations, but do this with the compassion one would give to a brother or sister. As leaders of businesses or households, we follow God's example when we spell out expectations and when we are compassionate when corrective action is required.

2 Thessalonians 3:14-15
And if any man obey not our word by this epistle, note that man, and have no company with him, that he may be ashamed. Yet count him not as an enemy, but admonish him as a brother.

Share best practices

Innovative employees often find a more efficient or safer way to do something when they are encouraged to do so by their leadership. This sounds simple but it works. I was able to save several million dollars by just asking associate managers in one subsidiary company what they could do to save money. They had good ideas, but they did not suggest the ideas because they thought management would not accept them.

The sum of all the ideas from associates constitutes the best practices for the organization. Best practices evolve with time since thoughtful people will improve upon them. Sharing the practices among the organization's associates helps everyone doing similar work to be more efficient, and this should be encouraged.

We can share best practices most efficiently with a communication system that allows associates easy access to the information. Computer programs, designed to allow best practice searches by function and task, allow everyone to participate who has access to a computer. Companies will often provide a place with a public computer that employees can log into to allow more people to share information. A central coordinator should review practices entered into the system library to ensure they meet guidelines for quality, safety, and function. Screen all best practices submitted since they may unknowingly violate a company practice for safety or quality. Information systems coupled with programs that encourage best practice reporting stimulate productivity improvement. Encouragement to share information breaks down the barriers of associates who protect their best practices to make them more competitive.

A study of comparative data for similar operations in an organization can lead to straightforward answers why some are doing better than others do. There is an emotional hurtle to cross however, when we assess best practice information. To implement a better practice, it is necessary to get over personal pride and acknowledge that someone else has better results. A progressive leader, especially one new in an organization, will use comparative data to understand where immediate improvements are possible to catch up with the internal competition. The newcomer will not focus solely to perform on a par with the competition. An aggressive leader will also create a parallel path to develop a vision and strategy to leap frog the competition and take performance leadership. Leaders can drown themselves in their own pride if they are not humble and do not acknowledge that someone else has a better way to do a task. They must act fast to catch up and not let pride stand in their way. Proverbs warns us against pride, which can lead to destruction.

Proverbs 16:18
Pride goeth before destruction and a haughty spirit before a fall.

This is a competitive world and the rewards go to leaders and associates who win by their contributions. Job encourages comparative data studies when he instructs us to seek from people around us knowledge that we can use.

Job 34:2-4

Hear my words, O ye wise men; and give ear unto me, ye that have knowledge. For the ear trieth words, as the mouth tasteth meat. Let us choose to us judgment: let us know among ourselves what is good.

Managing the Internal Process

Two shipping department workers who have not seen a customer order leave their dock in several days are listening to their employer deliver the annual business report. The employer's exuberance about current business performance and the future of the business would rival that of any itinerant preacher. One dock employee turns to other and says, "You cannot trust a thing he says but he sure makes you feel good." We have to maintain our values and conduct ourselves honestly with associates and customers even when things are not going well.

Maintain Christian values

"Are we there yet?" How we achieve goals is as important as the goal achievement. Guidelines for conduct are necessary that both challenge and develop the team. Businesses use value-based selling points that distinguish them from their competition. Some businesses develop points of distinction with the customer like honesty, trust, customer service, and partnership. Businesses can also develop points of distinction that speak to the customer's social values like community service, the respectful treatment of associates, and environmental protection. The achievement of financial goals should not be an "anything goes" exercise. Goal achievement must happen without negatively affecting team spirit, safety, quality or the reputation of the organization in the community. Values deal more with who we are as an organization versus how much money we can make. Hence, the evaluation of goal achievement should include both subjective and objective measures. For instance, did reducing waste disposal costs harm the environment? Leaders are the gatekeepers of the company values. Their judgment is critical to the evaluation process, and their tenacity to maintain values even in hard times will make or break the business. Proverbs tells us to keep an eye on the future but be careful to keep to the ways that establish strong values.

> **Proverbs 4:25-26**
> Let thine eyes look right on, and let thine eyelids look straight before thee. Ponder the path of thy feet, and let all thy ways be established.

Take corrective action
One of the key lessons to teach associates is that they should take action when they see a problem even when that problem may be in another person's area of responsibility. The action may be simply to notify the manager in charge of the area of the problem. In drastic situations, especially with issues that relate to quality or safety, the employees should be empowered to take immediate action to arrest the problem. This can mean empowering individuals to shut down an operation. Strategies cannot be fulfilled or key performance indicators (KPI's) achieved unless everyone participates and takes action to promptly correct issues. Problems that go unsolved are the seeds of destruction in an organization. The small problem or issue not resolved immediately can grow into a giant drain on the resources of the organization if it mushrooms into a more significant issue. Luke tells us that like the Good Samaritan, we should not walk by issues. We should be a force to help solve them.

> **Luke 10:30-35**
> And Jesus answering said, A certain man went down from Jerusalem to Jericho, and fell among thieves, which stripped him of his raiment, and wounded him, and departed, leaving him half dead. And by chance there came down a certain priest that way: and when he saw him, he passed by on the other side. And likewise a Levite, when he was at the place, came and looked on him, and passed by on the other side. But a certain Samaritan, as he journeyed, came where he was and when he saw him, he had compassion on him, And went to him, and bound up his wounds, pouring in oil and wine, and set him on his own beast, and brought him to an inn, and took care of him. And on the morrow when he departed, he took out two pence, and gave them to the host, and said unto him, Take care of him; and whatsoever thou spendest more, when I come again, I will repay thee.

Employees trained to solve problems are a valuable asset. When a problem occurs, there is usually pressure to solve it quickly before it causes too much personal or financial distress. It is important to instill discipline to understand what the problem is before a solution is implemented. Many times people jump to a conclusion without a proper examination of the facts and implement a solution that makes the problem worse rather than better. For instance, the good will gesture to send two replacements for a returned defective item may cause increased grief if both of the items sent are also defective. This type of fumbling performance can make a mildly irritated customer an enraged customer who searches the telephone book for a new supplier. We should train associates to take the time to understand and define problems before they propose solutions. Leaders should train associates to use professional problem-solving techniques to ensure the issue is resolved with the first attempt. The ability to help clients solve their problems in a professional manner is a positive competitive distinction. James tells us that problems we face can help us gain strength and maturity if we approach them in a positive manner and have the patience to work through them.

James 1:2-4
My brethren, count it all joy when ye fall into divers temptations; Knowing this, that the trying of your faith worketh patience. But let patience have her perfect work, that ye may be perfect and entire, wanting nothing.

Minimize process variation

An organization improves when it finds ways to "wow" its customers. Customers especially appreciate a consistent product or service. Achieve this by reducing quality variations caused by processes that are not well controlled. A consistent product or service allows customers to provide more consistency to their customers so they have fewer problems in their processes. Quality in means quality out is easier to achieve. Process variability reduction is important to this effort. A KPI on process variability is normally a required part of a team's progress review. Measure process variation with upper and lower control limit charts. These charts find use to control processes in the administrative, sales, and production areas. The charts show the upper and lower limits of acceptable performance. Actual performance plotted on the chart that is between the two limits quickly shows if the process is in control. When performance starts to go beyond the upper or lower control limits, quick action is required to address the variances. Institute goals to reduce variability and monitor performance with a KPI. Processes and procedures that have little variability are the most cost efficient. They produce the highest quality output with the least waste and inefficiency. As variability increases, the number of rejects, returns, customer complaints, and warranty costs go up.

"Don't buy it if it was made on Monday or Friday!" One of the greatest opportunities for process variation to creep into a system is at start up and shutdown of the work process. This is especially true after maintenance work is required because of a malfunction. After a shutdown period and then a startup, additional issues often are present to cause variability. In offices, long absences can cause an employee to forget procedures or procedural steps and make mistakes. Office equipment and systems may be slow to start up due to technical difficulties. In manufacturing systems, startup also introduces additional problems with machines and materials that can lead to variations in output. Once machines and processes run for a while they usually settle down and variability stabilizes. The startup problems can be a result of temperatures stabilizing, the operator's need to tune the machine, raw material variations or poor maintenance that needs correction. The ability to start up, changeover, and shutdown a process with minimum variability, waste and lost time is the hallmark of an excellent process whether it is in an office or factory environment. One simple way to improve start up efficiency is to have someone come in early to start the equipment and resolve issues before the entire office or factory staff arrives.

Customers help define the allowable control limits for process variability. Customers who faithfully use a product will quickly detect variations in consistency or quality by tests or by problems caused in their process. The variation customers detect may not affect their willingness to continue to purchase the product. However, it will raise a red warning flag in their minds if they can trust a product and make them more open to competitive products. Consequently, it is important to get customer feedback about your product's performance. The reputation won with a thousand good deeds can be lost with one disaster. Businesses must build in product and service quality with well-engineered processes. In Corinthians, we learn that a small thing can affect an entire batch of product. The same is true in organizations and factories unless we build in careful controls to catch the bad before it affects and destroys the whole.

> **1 Corinthians 5:6**
> Your glorying is not good. Know ye not that a little leaven leaveneth the whole lump?

Promote continuous improvement

A leader must create a mindset to look continuously for ways to improve. Continuous improvement has many goals. Associates are encouraged to generate ideas in all areas that reduce cost, improve quality and safety, generate new product ideas, improve customer care, and improve morale. These are but a few examples. Many companies use both suggestion systems and team challenge groups to encourage the generation of ideas. Continuous improvement team participation helps to improve morale and enthusiasm. Interaction in the team generates more ideas. The disciples encouraged continuous improvement by looking to the future to improve and to achieve God's plan.

> **Philippians 3:13**
> Brethren, I count not myself to have apprehended but this one thing I do, forgetting those things, which are behind, and reaching forth unto those things, which are before.

Excellent operations do not just happen by accident. Employees must be encouraged, trained, and rewarded to apply their talents to improve the business. Employees have an incentive to participate when we publicly reward and recognize their contributions. Celebrate improvements often to show appreciation for team successes and individual contributions. Continuous improvement never stops since the business world continues to evolve, and this creates new opportunities to improve. In Nehemiah, we read that the people built the protective wall around Jerusalem because they had a mind to get it done and not because management wanted it done. Create this need in people to improve and success will follow.

Nehemiah 4:6
So built we the wall; and all the wall was joined together unto the half thereof: for the people had a mind to work.

Create opportunities for customers

Building in quality often means using the latest technologies to enhance a product's appeal to the customer. Part of a team's work is to keep up to date on technologies that can improve a product or service. Customers always want to know what your business is doing for them today to make their lives easier. Leaders must keep an eye open and spend time on research to ensure they are not trying to sell vacuum tubes to computer manufacturers who need silicon chips. The best companies create new opportunities and drive the market with new ideas for clients that fulfill a need the clients may not have recognized. Joel tells us to wake up and see what new things are available to improve business and help customers. In good times, we do not want to get into a complacent stupor about the capabilities we have only to have an aggressive competitor steal our business.

Joel 1:5-6
Awake, ye drunkards, and weep; and howl, all ye drinkers of wine, because of the new wine, for it is cut off from your mouth. For a nation is come up upon my land, strong, and without number, whose teeth are the teeth of a lion, and he hath the cheek teeth of a great lion.

New methods or technologies can be a challenge to get to market quickly. Do not tarnish the organization's reputation and fumble the ball during implementation. This can occur most easily with a new product or service launch. Any change can lead to problems since product or service qualities critical to a particular customer might be unwittingly compromised. However, do not spend time and money to try to predict every problem, otherwise a new product launch will take too long and be prohibitively expensive. Competitors scan the market for new entries and move quickly to introduce similar products or services. Agile competitors can match and beat a new entry into some markets and grab your customers if a launch moves too slowly.

It is important to prepare contingency plans for potential critical problem areas. Hold meetings with customers to brainstorm for potential problems and then develop plans to circumvent them. Customers may have to increase inventories if there is a risk of a shutdown or adjust work schedules to allow time to make changes. Maintain frequent customer and organizational communications before and during implementation to detect problems. The combination of potential problem analysis, contingency plans, and good communications will mitigate problem damage severity and save face with the customer. Most customers will be sympathetic and understand that change may lead to problems as long as the problem does not significantly affect their bottom line or reputation.

Organizational Results

Leaders need to be part of the collaborative environment to facilitate change, but they cannot smother the energy of associates with too much attention.

Do not micromanage

Exodus reminds us that God, like stockholders, was not always patient with inaction and expected things to move forward. In Exodus, we hear God prodding Moses to get his people moving.

Exodus 14:15

And the Lord said unto Moses, Wherefore criest thou unto me? Speak unto the children of Israel, that they go forward:

Leaders have the responsibility to monitor progress and keep the organization focused to move forward. However, micromanagement of associates to whom you have delegated authority is counterproductive to progress. It frustrates enthusiastic employees who want to be trusted to get a job done. Associates have different needs when it comes to how much guidance they want. Some associates want minimal guidance. Explain the goals and resources available to them and then get out of the way. Others want to discuss progress and receive guidance more often. The leader must spend the time to understand and work with each personality type to maximize associate performance. In Deuteronomy, God shows us that He monitored the progress of His people who wandered the desert for forty years. He did not interfere often, but He kept watch over them to ensure they were in good health and had the resources, clothes and food needed to complete the journey.

Deuteronomy 8:4

Thy raiment waxed not old upon thee, neither did thy foot swell, these forty years.

Leaders have a tendency toward micromanagement. By nature, they have a high degree of urgency to accomplish tasks so they may want to check on progress too often. Morale is hurt if leaders jump into a situation before it is necessary to do so since associates feel less empowered. Leaders need to be patient and have faith in the people to whom they delegated authority. Paul reminds us in his letter to the Galatians that if we have courage and trust, we will prevail.

Galatians 6:9
And let us not be weary in well doing: for in due season we shall reap, if we faint not.

Reports must create action
Publish progress reports close to when events happen to improve the ability to stay on target. Performance that strays from its target for a long time before someone detects the problem, takes more time to correct. Public business reports, like income statements and balance sheets, are not effective for day-to-day process control. Accounting prepares these reports weeks after the events occur, and the reports do not allow for quick discovery and corrective action. These formal reports lack the detail or quick feedback required by decision makers to monitor product and service performance. Publishing KPI reports with urgency and speed is important to ensure quick and efficient decisions at all levels of the organization. Ezekiel reminds us that the watchman in any organization must be always alert and ready to react to issues that arise in the course of business. Timely information is the alert mechanism needed in business to create corrective action.

Ezekiel 33:2-3
Son of man, speak to the children of thy people, and say unto them, when I bring the sword upon a land, if the people of the land take a man of their coasts, and set him for their watchman: If when he seeth the sword come upon the land, he blow the trumpet, and warn the people;

We need to train associates to understand what they need to do with an unacceptable variance. Bypassed alerts are bad for business. Defective products or services produced when associates bypass alerts may find their way to customers and cause them to drop you as a supplier. Associates with the same information may take different corrective actions. They may see the variation but not understand what it means or how a corrective action they take may affect other areas. Agreed guidelines for variance resolution are important to achieve consistency in all parts of the business. This is especially true in multiple shift environments and rapidly growing businesses. Guideline training takes time so do not expect associates whose work schedule is full to train properly a new employee. Training associates in an aggressive business expansion period may require partnerships with local educational institutions or the development of an in house training school. These are commonly used techniques to teach consistent procedures. The course work developed for the training also serves as a reservoir of knowledge that can be scrutinized as part of the business' continuous improvement. Ezekiel reminds us that the failure to monitor warnings, like the signals we get from process variation reports, through disinterest or lack of knowledge may lead to a self-imposed disaster.

Ezekiel 33:4
Then whosoever heareth the sound of the trumpet, and taketh not warning; if the sword come, and take him away, his blood shall be upon his own head.

Monitor competitors

Most businesses do not have a monopoly for their goods or services. Competition preys on unguarded businesses. Luke warns leaders to always be alert and assume a thief is coming to steal their treasure. Being proactive to prepare defenses is a leader's duty.

Luke 12:39
And this know, that if the goodman of the house had known what hour the thief would come, he would have watched, and not have suffered his house to be broken through.

Competition has the profit driven compulsion to go after successful businesses and segment the market by offering similar or better products and services. Monitor competitive action to identify who is trying to grab your business and which competitor's business is worth pursuing. Doing comparative reviews with your competition will highlight both the best and worse in your organization's performance. KPI's that are compared to the competition need to be broad in nature but focused in quantity since it is difficult information to get. Luke tells us to be vigilant. We might feel secure with the defenses we have built but there is always a potentially stronger opponent lurking nearby who can overcome us.

Luke 11:21-22
When a strong man armed keepeth his palace, his goods are in peace: But when a stronger than he shall come upon him, and overcome him, he taketh from him all his armour wherein he trusted, and divideth his spoils.

Develop partnerships

The specialized talents and technologies required to serve customers well are difficult, if not impossible, to develop internally in a rapidly growing organization. Growth through partnerships in today's world is a necessity. The selection of outside partners takes special skills to understand how a new partner can move the organization forward. Partnership development can be a full time job depending on the size of the business because as the business grows, partnership requirements can change. Some organizations acquire technology or expertise through acquisition. However, the financial and cultural integration strain from acquisitions does not always make for an attractive payback. Acquisitions are very time consuming to complete and may divert too much attention from the core business unless they are properly organized and staffed. Negotiating exclusive rights to use a supplier's patents, technologies, or expertise is sometimes a less expensive alternative. Successful partnerships over time can lead to successful acquisitions of the partners. Partnerships limit the ability of competitors to match results by denying them access to expertise or technologies.

Mark describes how Jesus encouraged partnership because of the supportive strength it provides when two work together. He sent out His disciples in pairs to preach to the world.

Mark 6:7
And he called unto him the twelve, and began to send them forth by two and two; and gave them power over unclean spirits;

Prepare for a crisis

To have a good year, a leader is always prepared for a bad year. A year full of good results can suddenly turn into a disaster if a crisis occurs. Preparation can make a crisis a bump in the road versus a drive off a cliff. Matthew warns us to be ready for the unexpected coming of the Lord. We should use this lesson to remind us to prepare for an unexpected crisis.

Matthew 24:42-44
Watch therefore: for ye know not what hour your Lord doth come. But know this that if the good man of the house had known in what watch the thief would come, he would have watched, and would not have suffered his house to be broken up. Therefore be ye also ready: for in such an hour as ye think not the Son of man cometh.

Disaster response plans will assure both associates and customers of a continuation of income if a serious problem occurs. Response plans typically include planned responses for medical emergencies, serious customer complaints, product recalls, natural disasters, bad press reports, unplanned facility shut downs, supplier or transportation interruptions, computer crashes, loss of electronic communications, and threats to either people or property. A crisis management team is necessary to establish in large businesses to address these and many more potential crisis issues. In a small business or household, the need to be prepared is no less great but the burden falls on fewer people.

Update crisis response plans annually to ensure that critical contact information has not changed and that the response team member lists are current. Do not be embarrassed to find that an emergency contact person or telephone number is not accurate in the middle of a crisis. Select an offsite command location as a rally point for management to gather if the home site is not accessible. Equip the offsite location with communications, copies of response plans, and information that is necessary to manage the crisis and continue business.

In this age of "24/7" news, a person who is trained to communicate with the news media is a critical member of a response team. Defuse a crisis panic in the minds of the public and the stockholders with a first response that is accurate and reassures them that appropriate measures are in place for a recovery. Urgency is important because news reporters may exaggerate a small crisis out of proportion while they wait for a response. News reporters know how to ask tough questions that at times are hard to respond to with an answer that reassures customers. For instance, a reporter may ask for a response to a question like, "Your Company advertises it has excellent product protection programs but you produce defective products and this incident is an example." Do not put an untrained person in front of a reporter. News reporters also have deadlines to make. They appreciate cooperation and are more willing to use your input if they get a quick response when they call. Obviously, the seriousness of these communications dictates that the business should have a primary and backup respondent available in a crisis. Many companies contract with lawyers trained to handle news media questions as their official spokespersons.

Stay focused on God

Leaders can get easily lost in plans, numbers, and problems and forget that the force behind their success is God's help. They must not lose faith in what they are doing, and they must be persistent in their request for God's help. Seeking God's help should be at the top of your to do list each day. In Matthew's gospel, he points out how the persistent, albeit diplomatic woman got her way with Jesus. Jesus played the part of a disinterested person to teach us a lesson. The message is clear that we need to be persistent in the prayers we make and have faith that God will help us.

Matthew 15:22-28
And, behold, a woman of Canaan came out of the same coasts, and cried unto him, saying, Have mercy on me, O Lord, thou Son of David; my daughter is grievously vexed with a devil. But he answered her not a word. And his disciples came and besought him, saying, Send her away; for she crieth after us. But he answered and said, I am not sent but unto the lost sheep of the house of Israel. Then came she and worshipped him, saying, Lord, help me. But he answered and said, It is not meet to take the children's bread, and to cast it to dogs. And she said, Truth, Lord: yet the dogs eat of the crumbs which fall from their masters' table. Then Jesus answered and said unto her, O woman, great is thy faith: be it unto thee even as thou wilt. And her daughter was made whole from that very hour.

If we submit to God's will, He will empower us to lead because He will fulfill His will through us. We are His hands and eyes on this earth to do His work. God calls us to empower people, provide education, and foster high morale. In Matthew's Gospel, he tells the story how Peter started out with great faith and had success, but he became worried and fearful, lost faith, and nearly drowned. He rallied himself and asked for Jesus' help and he received it. We need to remind ourselves in times of trouble that God will never abandon us; we just have to ask for help.

Matthew 14:23-31
And when he had sent the multitudes away, he went up into a mountain apart to pray: and when the evening was come, he was there alone. But the ship was now in the midst of the sea, tossed with waves: for the wind was contrary. And in the fourth watch of the night Jesus went unto them, walking on the sea. And when the

disciples saw him walking on the sea, they were troubled, saying, It is a spirit; and they cried out for fear. But straightway Jesus spake unto them, saying, Be of good cheer; it is I; be not afraid. And Peter answered him and said, Lord, if it be thou, bid me come unto thee on the water. And he said, Come. And when Peter was come down out of the ship, he walked on the water, to go to Jesus. But when he saw the wind boisterous, he was afraid; and beginning to sink, he cried, saying, Lord, save me. And immediately Jesus stretched forth his hand, and caught him, and said unto him, O thou of little faith, wherefore didst thou doubt? And when they were come into the ship, the wind ceased. Then they that were in the ship came and worshipped him, saying, Of a truth thou art the Son of God.

Most importantly, leaders must allow everyone to share in the rewards of their labor. This stimulates morale. Ecclesiastic's tells that we should enjoy the work we do and enjoy its rewards.

Ecclesiastes 3:13
And also that every man should eat and drink, and enjoy the good of all his labour, it is the gift of God.

Human Resource Development

Human resources (HR) role is like the role that the prophet Isaiah saw as his noble mission on earth.

> **Isaiah 61:1**
> The spirit of the Lord God is upon me; because the Lord hath anointed me to preach good tidings unto the meek; he hath sent me to bind up the brokenhearted, to proclaim liberty to the captives, and the opening of the prison to them that are bound;

Associates who work in HR have a unique opportunity to help people. The HR staff must deal with the day-to-day work of benefits administration, but their primary focus is to develop programs that make the employees' work easier to do. HR must extend help to assist with personal problems that cause associates to have low work performance. Employees are more dedicated and work harder when they believe the business has their personal welfare at heart.

Develop a common business language

HR personnel can fulfill Isaiah's mission if they are effective with communications. Communications can liberate minds from fear, free people to be productive, and deliver good news about the benefits to work hard for the business. HR must help the organization develop a common language and freedom of expression that encourages everyone to communicate across all borders, cultures, and countries. Genesis's story emphasizes that a common language creates common thinking and has great unifying power. Unfortunately, in this case, the people used the strength of a common language against God's will when they set their minds to build the Tower of Babel.

> **Genesis 11:6**
> And the Lord said, Behold, the people is one, and they have all one language; and this they begin to do: and now nothing will be restrained from them, which they have imagined to do.

In the business world, a common language refers to terminologies and procedures that aid communication. As an example, the computer industry has a worldwide terminology understood in all languages. Bytes, bits, gigs, and RAM are the same terms the world over. A common language refers to certain words or to the names given to certain processes and programs that are universal to the business. It can also refer to how associates refer to each other. This is especially true with quality and safety programs that get catchy names like *Zero Defects*, which draw attention to the purpose of the program. The terms *red train* for anger and aggression, and *green train* for sensible conduct, are code words to train staff with anger management. Associates can warn their peers in a non-aggressive manner that they are too aggressive by telling them that they are on the *red train* and they need to get on the *green train*. God placed such great value on communications that the Holy Spirit personally enabled it with the apostles. Acts tells us how God sent the Holy Spirit to give the gift of languages to the apostles so that everyone understood them.

Acts 2:1-8
And when the day of Pentecost was fully come, they were all with one accord in one place. And suddenly there came a sound from heaven as of a rushing mighty wind, and it filled all the house where they were sitting. And there appeared unto them cloven tongues like as of fire, and it sat upon each of them. And they were all filled with the Holy Ghost, and began to speak with other tongues, as the Spirit gave them utterance. And there were dwelling at Jerusalem Jews, devout men, out of every nation under heaven. Now when this was noised abroad, the multitude came together, and were confounded, because that every man heard them speak in his own language. And they were all amazed and marveled, saying one to another, Behold, are not all these which speak Galilaeans? And how hear we every man in our own tongue, wherein we were born?

Use words that evoke pictures
Successful communication programs use common language words that evoke thoughts and pictures in people's minds. Single words and short

phrases can evoke and summarize complex thoughts and philosophies and quickly bring people to focus during discussions. For instance, a catchy name placed on a complex program helps the listener to recognize the topic discussed and brings to mind background information previously learned. The catchy name is like a label on a file folder that is full of background information.

Developing program names and terminology is a major undertaking. Do this in parallel with the development of the entire strategy and goal planning effort to help deliver the message, promote understanding, and aid retention. Catchy program names like *Safety First* or *Go Green* can evoke in a person's mind a broad list of rules and procedures about the program's application. Strategies and goals are easier to accomplish if they are in the forefront of people's minds and well-designed program names help to remind employees to stay focused.

Common terminology used across the entire organization also promotes shared best practices. Provide translated documents in the local language to help everyone understand shared documents. However, it is possible to use key phrases like *Safety First* or *Zero Defects* without translation once the local staff understands what these terms mean. International associates are often keen to learn English terms as it makes them feel part of the global team. In the book of Ester, we hear how early kings who ruled vast empires from a central location found it important to communicate common rules and procedures in the native languages of their vast kingdoms.

Esther 1:1-2, 22
Now it came to pass in the days of Ahasuerus, (this is Ahasuerus which reigned, from India even unto Ethiopia, over an hundred and seven and twenty provinces:) That in those days, when the king Ahasuerus sat on the throne of his kingdom, which was in Shushan the palace. For he sent letters into all the king's provinces, into every province according to the writing thereof, and to every people after their language, that every man should bear rule in

his own house, and that it should be published according to the language of every people.

Words and phrases may have different meanings around the world. Translations are sometimes impossible to make that give the same meaning or impact that they have in the native language. The international nature of most business requires care in the selection and use of terminology since translated words or phrases can cause offense or embarrassment. In addition, a review of copyrighted words and phrases ensures the business does not waste money to redo a communication program because of a copyright infringement. A classic example of the need to check local interpretations is the name of a former Chevrolet car, the Nova. In Spanish, "no va" means do not go which is not a message about cars that a company wants to deliver to Latin American customers.

Share business information

Discontent with communications is usually the biggest complaint in employee morale surveys. Complaints are typically about managers who do not communicate plans, poor information flow between departments or conflicts between people. If left unaddressed, communication problems can cause poor morale and a loss of trust. This discontent will grow exponentially as more people find that they have it as a common problem, and the anger will be especially intense if management does not respond to the problem. As Paul notes in his letter to the Galatians, a seemingly little thing can affect the entire mass. A problem not addressed is like the leaven in bread. It can cause a small communication issue to grow into a large issue that affects the whole organization.

Galatians 5:9
A little leaven leaveneth the whole lump.

Human Resources act as a funnel through which associate information passes. HR needs to develop employee trust to keep the funnel free flowing. Open communications surface issues quickly for resolution before the issues can fester and infect the organization. Management's resolve to improve communications dictates a program's success. Issues answered quickly and information shared with employees about business status, especially financial information, opens the gate to greater trust and productivity. Leaders who fail to understand that productivity improves with an effective communication infrastructure will not support it and they will fail.

Managers sometimes fear that if they share information with employees they will give away secret company strategies that may fall into a competitor's hands or it may cause the employees to demand more from a profitable company. These are bad excuses not to share information. It is far better to have knowledgeable employees who fight for success than ones who flounder in the dark and who do not feel secure about the direction or financial status of the company. In Numbers, we read about the discontent that builds in people when they feel a lack of communications from their leader. Leaders need to reassure their associates by sharing information to reinforce the vision for the future so that associates can get through difficult times.

Numbers 14:2
And all the children of Israel murmured against Moses and against Aaron: and the whole congregation said unto them, Would God that we had died in the land of Egypt! or would God we had died in this wilderness!

Another reason leaders may not share information is that information ownership is a form of power. They feel they have more control and influence with ownership even though hoarding information can be harmful to the business. Leaders need to overcome this mentality of control and help people win. Nothing stays hidden forever, and eventually, leaders who hide information will lose the trust and support of their employees. I left my first job as an engineer after a local newspaper reported my Company location was going to down size. The Company managers did not inform us before the newspaper article, and they did not effectively communicate afterwards. This destroyed my faith in them and I quickly left the company along with others who also felt insecure about their futures. The Company may have retained talented personnel if they did not hide information. Matthew reminds us that all hidden facts will be revealed.

> **Matthew 10:26**
> Fear them not therefore: for there is nothing covered, that shall not be revealed; and hid, that shall not be known.

Recruit the best people

New personnel inject lifeblood into the organization to keep it alive. People are necessary to do the work of the organization to make it grow and prosper. Leaders realize that profitable opportunities abound in the world to provide products and services. However, they cannot reap the benefits unless they have a highly trained and qualified staff to help with the harvest. In today's world, quality is as important as quantity. Many firms find they need to import educated employees or export work to other countries since locally trained and talented people are too few or do not exist. Matthew emphasizes the point using Christ's words that without people there is no harvest.

> **Matthew 9:37**
> Then saith he unto his disciples, The harvest truly is plenteous, but the labourers are few;

Align recruitment with the organizational strategy and goals. The competencies needed to make the changes that achieve the business plan may not be available with the current staff. Consequently, it is necessary to recruit new skills to make the changes happen that will bring the organization into the future. Most current employees will accept changes and personnel additions when leaders discuss these things beforehand and show how the changes tie in with the business plan. However, associates are demoralized and feel insecure when a stranger shows up unannounced. Leaders need to train new staff members about the company's history and culture to ensure the new people have a smooth entry into the team.

Respect for the company's history reduces conflict with senior employees and improves teamwork.

Training reduces stress

Train people to cope with managing change, and it will reduce their stress level and improve performance. Most people dislike change because the stress draws energy away from doing a good job. Change is fundamental to improvement and change without training support is doomed to failure. We hear from Proverbs about the importance to train associates and the confidence and growth it offers.

> **Proverbs 1:2-5**
> To know wisdom and instruction; to perceive the words of understanding; To receive the instruction of wisdom, justice, and judgment, and equity; To give subtlety to the simple, to the young man knowledge and discretion. A wise man will hear, and will increase learning; and a man of understanding shall attain unto wise counsels.

Group instructional sessions like those given to large assemblies of people can be impersonal and leave people cold to the message. Individuals are the focus of attention and the program needs to reach each individual. Use breakout sessions to break large groups into smaller ones to discuss the material presented in the assembly. This ensures that each individual has the opportunity to ask questions and provide quality feedback to improve the training. Every manager and meeting facilitator must be able to conduct these small group sessions and communicate well. Unfortunately, schools and universities train people for the technical skills of their jobs, but students are not, in most cases, trained to be effective communicators. Consequently, designated personnel need training to facilitate meetings. Conduct this training in parallel with the training program development.

Individual records of employee training are necessary to ensure that everyone has the required job skills and that no one has missed a required session. Sessions should have attendance sheets that each employee signs to prove attendance. Vacations and unplanned emergencies may cause an associate to miss an important training class. HR must develop a list of training needs for each job and monitor the list to ensure everyone's training needs are current. This is especially important for equal employment opportunity, discrimination, quality, safety, and environmental training. Employees not properly trained in these areas may put the business at risk of government fines or lawsuits. Government agencies will demand to see training documentation for each individual, and they may wish to interview privately selected employees. Employees who took a training class several months back may tell an inspector they never had the class because of a memory lapse. This makes their signatures on a class attendance sheet a mandatory piece of documentation to maintain. Businesses win or lose injury lawsuits based on their ability to show documentation that they trained associates to use proper procedures.

It is common to base a person's promotion solely on the ability to perform the new position's technical requirements and a history of success in former jobs. However, a person who has held many jobs and each for a short period can show success if business conditions were favorable. A strong record of accomplishment over a long period of time during which there were both favorable and adverse conditions is a better way to judge a person for promotion. Good management development programs give individuals change management challenges that increase with difficulty as the individuals show positive results with the skills they learned. It is important to keep records of the proficiency with which individuals accomplish these challenges to guide succession plans. Psalms reminds us that God tested people whom He trained.

Psalms 66:10
For thou, O God, hast proved us: thou hast tried us, as silver is tried.

Recognize and reward associate skills

Many companies develop dual paths of advancement and rewards to recognize both individuals who have high technical skill proficiency and people who have the organization, communication, and people skills required in management. Dual path reward programs are excellent motivators. They recognize both managerial and technical skills and minimize feelings of poor compensation especially with the technically skilled group. Recognition programs should include both title and compensation levels for each group to advance through. Titles and job benefits, like a private office or reserved parking space, are a greater motivation to some people than money since it recognizes their stature in their specialty. In some organizations, highly qualified people like scientists and technicians get salaries commensurate with or higher than their direct managers do. It takes mature managers to understand and recognize the value of highly paid experts to the success of the business and their own careers. We all are equal in God's eyes; we just have different responsibilities and talents.

Plan for your replacement

An organization is nothing without the right people to run it and work in it. This makes succession planning a critical part of management's responsibility. In Deuteronomy, we hear how Moses recognized the need to find a successor after God prompted him.

> <u>Deuteronomy 31:1-2, 7</u>
> And Moses went and spake these words unto all Israel. And he said unto them, I am an hundred and twenty years old this day; I can no more go out and come in: also the Lord hath said unto me, Thou shalt not go over this Jordan. And Moses called unto Joshua, and said unto him in the sight of all Israel, Be strong and of a good courage: for thou must go with this people unto the land which the Lord hath sworn unto their fathers to give them; and thou shalt cause them to inherit it.

Moses' story shows that it is difficult for people who have worked many years to build an organization to turn it over to someone else and walk away. You leave behind more than your labors; you leave behind a part of your life. This is especially true of leaders who are about to retire and have enjoyed the personal rewards, attention and benefits of their work and look to a vast unknown before them. In Moses' case, he required direct intervention from God to name a successor. Company boards do the same with the management they advise. In Ecclesiastes, we see how a leader fretted over the decision to find a successor and how it affected his work until he realized his desire to keep hold was just vanity.

Ecclesiastes 2:17-19
Therefore I hated life; because the work that is wrought under the sun is grievous unto me: for all is vanity and vexation of spirit. Yea, I hated all my labour which I had taken under the sun: because I should leave it unto the man that shall be after me. And who knoweth whether he shall be a wise man or a fool? Yet shall he have rule over all my labour wherein I have laboured, and wherein I have shewed myself wise under the sun. This is also vanity.

Choosing a successor does not mean that we have less value to the organization or the greater community we live in. In fact, God tells us in Psalms that people who follow His path will lead long, energetic, and useful lives. Corinthians tells us that even though the outside shell may grow old, the inside person can be continually renewed.

Psalms 92:13-14
Those that be planted in the house of the Lord shall flourish in the courts of our God. They shall still bring forth fruit in old age; they shall be fat and flourishing;

2 Corinthians 4:16
For which cause we faint not; but though our outward man perish, yet the inward man is renewed day by day.

Review succession plans annually

Annual succession plan reviews are an important part of management's responsibility. It not only addresses the development needs for current employees but it also identifies future leaders who may be needed to replace highly skilled staff who will retire, have serious health issues that bench them, or decide to move on to better opportunities. Losing a key player without a worthy replacement destroys customer, stakeholder, and stockholder confidence. A strong leadership team enhances the value of a company's stock when it has depth in its management and technical ranks. This gives investors' confidence in the future of the company to grow and prosper.

Build a diverse organization

Succession plans must address diversity. Diversity is not a majority – minority issue. Diversity helps to build stronger teams. In the book of Daniel, we hear how a king used diversity to strengthen his team when he recruited Israelites to train with the children of his followers.

> **Daniel 1:3-5**
> And the king spake unto Ashpenaz the master of his eunuchs, that he should bring certain of the children of Israel, and of the king's seed, and of the princes; Children in whom was no blemish, but well favoured, and skillful in all wisdom, and cunning in knowledge, and understanding science, and such as had ability in them to stand in the king's palace, and whom they might teach the learning and the tongue of the Chaldeans. And the king appointed them a daily provision of the king's meat, and of the wine which he drank: so nourishing them three years, that at the end thereof they might stand before the king.

Organizational design needs to include a mix of backgrounds and different perspectives to encourage creativity and innovation. A diverse organization is more sensitive to the markets it serves since it has a mix of staff that represents customers in the markets served. The Managing Director of our Company in Nairobi, Kenya emphasized this lesson to me during an assignment there to recruit a manager for his production facility. It was a lesson in creating a diverse organization in an international setting. I thought the population in Kenya was homogeneous enough that cultural diversity would not be a challenge, but I was wrong. The Director was concerned that he had too many members of the *Kikuyu* tribe on his management team. The *Kikuyu* is the largest tribe in Kenya. He wanted if possible to recruit people from other Kenyan tribes so his organization better reflected the population cross section of the country. This recruitment lesson taught me that diversity has many forms.

Diverse organizations bring people together who challenge each other with different perspectives and personality types that can generate new ideas. It takes a good manager to funnel the creative energies of a peppery, diverse group into a productive team that will yield a benefit to the business. Meetings often produce a lot of talk but no useful results. A good meeting facilitator presents worthwhile challenges to the group and guides the discussion to generate ideas for improvement. Bland organizations that lack diversity of thought will yield little improvement. An organization can stimulate new thinking by the use of special projects that bring together internal associates with diverse backgrounds. The special projects may be to start a new program, like continuous improvement, or launch a new product or service. In Romans, we hear how diversity brings different gifts to the organization.

<u>Romans 12:6</u>
Having then gifts differing according to the grace that is given to us, whether prophecy, let us prophesy according to the proportion of faith;

Train people to interview job candidates

A well-structured recruitment process gets the diverse staff and skills that a business needs for success. Train staff members to interview new candidates. Each person in the interview process plays a particular role like the pieces on a chessboard. Define each role before the interview to avoid conflicts. The questions asked need to follow a general framework so the interviewers can compare notes on each candidate. This is especially true when they interview several candidates over a period of several days or even weeks. In this situation, it is not possible to do fair interviews of several candidates for the same job unless there is an interview outline and interviewers make written notes of their questions and the answers they receive. Devote time to the interview. Read the resumé beforehand along with your question list and the job description. Managers who rush from a meeting to do an interview without preparation time cannot do a good interview. They give the person being interviewed a bad impression of the company as they stumble through paperwork and questions.

Carefully prepared job descriptions are tedious to write, but they are the checklist against which new team members are hired. All interviewers should agree on the job description requirements and the priority of the skill levels desired. HR has the job to ensure the job description meets all legal requirements including the physical capabilities required for the job. These may include the weight a worker must lift or the ability to drive or fly to meetings. Managers also need to step back and look at how individuals will fit into the whole team to see if everyone will work well together and not just look at individual competencies. Paul gives us direction that diverse team members must share their individual gifts with one another to create a line of one.

1 Corinthians 12:12
For as the body is one, and hath many members, and all the members of that one body, being many, are one body: so also is Christ.

The interview must determine if the candidate is a person willing to compromise for the good of the team. A person who is highly skilled but cannot be effective as a team player is not a good investment. Highly opinionated people who cannot appreciate other perspectives beyond their own thoughts can do more harm than good despite their technical expertise. It is very difficult to remove employees once they are hired. A poor hire can do a lot of damage to team morale. This makes the interviewing process very critical since so much of a company's success depends on the people they hire. Paul says that each team member must be a servant to the other team members.

1 Corinthians 9:19
For though I be free from all men, yet have I made myself servant unto all, that might gain the more.

Drive out the fear of failure

Confident team members create energy that can speed progress like a nuclear chain reaction. Release employee energy by driving out the fear of failure or embarrassment. This can be a real or imagined fear. Associates who always look over their shoulder for fear of criticism will not be enthusiastic to try new methods. The fear of criticism will cause associates to be slow to fulfill their responsibilities as they watch every step they make. These are difficult barriers to overcome. Leaders will achieve credibility when they back their direction with consistent actions that reinforce confidence in associates. Associates at work and the family at home mimic a leader's actions. Associates test leaders every day on their consistency of action. It is critical that leaders match their words with their actions. Proverbs tells us that people who work with unselfish actions to promote a good environment will also prosper.

Proverbs 11:24-25
There is that scattereth, and yet increaseth; and there is that withholdeth more than is meet, but it tendeth to poverty. The liberal soul shall be made fat: and he that watereth shall be watered also himself.

Use equitable performance reviews

Individual performance appraisals need to be trustworthy. Succession plans need as a base an appraisal process that is fair and equitable across the organization and based on standard review principles. Larger global businesses need a more formalized and consistent review process to gain trust. Promotions and transfers are frequently determined from performance evaluations, so they must be trustworthy.

Even in standardized performance rating systems, fairness requires that managers have some latitude in their ability to rate employees. Changes occur constantly throughout the year and a person's performance toward goals in any one year may not be entirely within that person's control. Business environment changes, family issues or a health crisis can affect the performance of the best employee. Consequently, managers need some flexibility in the evaluation process to account for these changing dynamics as long as they adequately document the reasons for the variance.

Variances are possible to measure only if there is a baseline plan in place at the beginning of the review period. A plan makes it easier for the manager to consul employees throughout the year and to keep them on track. The fierce winds of competition may alter the ambitious plans set at the beginning of the year. Even small market changes may affect business plans. James illustrates this point when he tells us that a small helm can change the direction of a large ship.

James 3:4
Behold also the ships, which though they be so great, and are driven of fierce winds, yet are they turned about with a very small helm, whithersoever the governor listeth.

James also emphasizes the need for a supervisor to listen with patience and judge with compassion when changes affect an employee's performance.

James 1:19
Wherefore, my beloved brethren, let every man be swift to hear, slow to speak, slow to wrath:

Human Resources have the unique challenge to coach managers to use the employee review process and the company's compensation program to improve performance. Associates monitor the performance of their fellow employees to see if there is equal treatment in the review and reward system. I have seen instances where employees in the same job class became distressed when their pay increases were different from their peers by less than ten cents per hour. The money was not the issue. Their pride and their opinion of equal treatment was the issue. Leaders need clear guidelines to issue merit increases. Managers who use the review process to give financial rewards to promote loyalty and to protect their kingdoms destroy morale. They push back on standardized performance programs that stress pay for performance since these programs do not permit unfair favoritism and rewards. Leaders have a great responsibility to be fair. A leadership position is a gift from God. Leaders cannot survive if they reward only loyalty and forsake performance. God expects leaders to rule well and to be servants to the team.

James 3:1
My brethren, be not many masters, knowing that we shall receive the greater condemnation.

Communicate expectations to employees

"I was supposed to do what?" Effective organizations align goals with their strategic plan to set clear expectations for their employees. These expectations include not only the objective results, usually defined by numbers, but also the subjective results related to how employees perform and interact as communicators, innovators, problem solvers, and team members. One on one, sit down discussions between managers and employees to discuss and document expectations is critical to align employee and business performance. There is a huge benefit to this investment of time. Employees who agree to their goals will be more committed to achieve them. Without the investment of time, time that is never easy to find, progress will be less, and there can be considerable frustration created during performance reviews. Managers must be sensitive to the needs of their employees and give them the straightforward advice and guidance Paul recommends.

1 Thessalonians 5:14
Now we exhort you, brethren, warn them that are unruly, comfort the feebleminded, support the weak, be patient toward all men.

Set up a calendar of dates for formal and informal progress reviews to keep track of changes so there is better accountability. Associates will work on goals more intently when they know a review is coming up in a few weeks. Regular reviews ensure that the original plans have not changed, the employees are working on the expectations, and they have adequate resources to complete the job. Distractions constantly bombard the staff. It is easy for them to get off course and even lose sight of the original expectations. When this happens, counsel employees to get them back on track. Leaders, managers, and supervisors need to keep records of each associate's positive and negative performance events during the year. They need to reinforce the associate's positive contributions and to make corrections to expectations at appropriate intervals. The associate's progress will determine if the interval between reviews is lengthened or shortened. The goal is to ensure that there are no performance rating surprises at the associate's year-end evaluation. Matthew gives us guidance that the leader must keep track of the flock and not lose even one.

Matthew 18:12
How think ye? If a man have an hundred sheep, and one of them be gone astray, doth he not leave the ninety and nine, and goeth into the mountains, and seeketh that which is gone astray?

Leaders must treat associates as equals, not favoring anyone during the review process, and giving all associates equal counsel to help them succeed. In Romans, Paul tells us equal access and counsel is important to ensure all parts of the organization succeed.

Romans 9:21
Hath not the potter power over the clay, of the same lump to make one vessel unto honour, and another unto dishonour?

Discipline to improve performance

Disciplining employees who do not meet expectations is not what managers like to do. Expectations can be goal related or personal, like attendance, tardiness, language, and abusive or prejudicial treatment of fellow employees. It is more fun and less stressful to give praise, salary increases, and promotions. Managers often avoid disciplining employees simply because they do not have the courage to do it, or they gloss over the problems and the associate thinks everything is fine. This is not fair to the employee. No one likes to deliver bad news, but it is necessary to do so if an organization expects to maintain discipline, help people to be successful, and achieve its long-term goals. Apply the three C's to make disciplining employees easier to do. The three C's are first: compliment positive performance aspects. This sets a positive tone for the meeting. Second, coach to correct the performance deficiency including possible penalties if performance does not improve. Be honest and sincere. Third, conclude with positive comments about the future if performance improves. This puts associates in a positive frame of mind that the future will be brighter if they improve. The Bible encourages us to discipline others when they do not carry their fair share of the load.

> **2 Thessalonians 3:6-16**
> Now we command you, brethren, in the name of our Lord Jesus Christ, that ye withdraw yourselves from every brother that walketh disorderly, and not after the tradition which he received of us. For yourselves know how ye ought to follow us: for we behaved not ourselves disorderly among you; Neither did we eat any man's bread for naught; but wrought with labour and travail night and day, that we might not be chargeable to any of you: Not because we have not power, but to make ourselves an example unto you to follow us. For even when we were with you, this we commanded you, that if any would not work, neither should he eat. For we hear that there are some which walk among you disorderly, working not at all, but are busybodies. Now them that are such we command and exhort by our Lord Jesus Christ, that with quietness they

work, and eat their own bread. But ye, brethren, be not weary in well doing. And if any man obey not our word by this epistle, note that man, and have no company with him, that he may be ashamed. Yet count him not as an enemy, but admonish him as a brother. Now the Lord of peace himself give you peace always by all means. The Lord be with you all.

Associates expect leaders to discipline people who do not meet the criteria that the associates faithfully follow. Employees also feel that fairness dictates that leaders enforce rules. Associates will not necessarily complain about fellow employees, but they do expect managers to be attentive and catch violations. Lack of action on management's part leads employees to say, "If they don't care, I don't care." This attitude kills employee innovation and creative participation in the company's work.

Employees have the responsibility to accept the disciplinary advice and implement the recommendations they are given. This requires them to trust that management has their best interest in mind. Rebellious employees, who consistently disregard advice, are a liability. It is very important to document the behavior of employees who do not meet expectations and who do not respond to advice. If termination is necessary, there must be proof that the employee had adequate counsel and warning. Some managers request the employee to sign a copy of the disciplinary notice as proof that the conversation took place. It is advisable to review all potential employee discharges with an attorney. It is money well spent that will avoid expensive legal mistakes. Fellow employees may agree that a person deserves termination, but they still want that employee to get repeated warnings and a fair chance to reform. Employees see the disciplined employee's treatment as an example of their treatment in a similar situation. Knowing they will have adequate warning if they stray from expectations helps to build confidence and drives out fear of failure. Proverbs sums up these lessons on employee behavior in a few words.

Proverbs 10:16-17
The labour of the righteous tendeth to life: the fruit of the wicked to sin. He is in the way of life that keepeth instruction: but he that refused reproof erred.

Ethical Behavior

Two men try to outbid each other for an exceptional English countryside painting. One man finally bids ten thousand dollars forcing the other man to concede. Afterwards, the auctioneer asks the winning bidder if obtaining the painting was his greatest wish. No says the man, my greatest wish is that I had the ten thousand dollars. This joke reminds us to adhere to the standards of honest conduct.

Honesty is the foundation to build on

Matthew points out to us that we have to get priorities right and not overlook improprieties of honesty and justice while we strive to improve profitability and performance.

> **Matthew 23:23-24**
> Woe unto you, scribes and Pharisees, hypocrites! For ye pay tithe of mint and anise and cumin, and have omitted the weightier matters of the law, judgment, mercy, and faith: these ought ye to have done, and not to leave the other undone. Ye blind guides, which strain at a gnat, and swallow a camel

Avoid improprieties

Honesty and ethical practice is a necessity at every level in an organization. Whether at home or at work, people we serve demand it from us. Avoid even the appearance of inappropriate action. Expose inappropriate actions and make immediate corrections. Cover-ups are usually exposed, and it will make the event even worse. Admit to your mistakes and explain what you learned from them. This promotes a culture of honesty and trust. People like to forgive leaders who confess and quickly make amends, but they remember and mistrust forever a leader who lies to them. If you do not want to see your action as a headline in the local newspaper, do not do it. In Paul's letter to the Thessalonians, there is a message about punishment when we do not adhere to honest interaction.

1 Thessalonians 4:6, 5-22
That no man go beyond and defraud his brother in any matter: because that the Lord is the avenger of all such, as we also have forewarned you and testified. Abstain from all appearance of evil.

There are unscrupulous people who start out with the intention to deceive and who knowingly do illegal acts to gain profits for themselves. They have no feeling of remorse for the people they hurt. However, many people caught in dishonest acts did not start with the intention to be dishonest or hurt others. During the normal course of business, there may be enticing offers that have questionable legality. These might relate to tax dodges, price fixing, purchasing illegal goods, or passing off faulty materials. If accepted, these initial offers will slowly draw the leader into deeper and deeper compromises that lead down the road to destruction. James reminds us that we will all be tempted and we must resist it.

James 1:14-15
But every man is tempted, when he is drawn away of his own lust, and enticed. Then when lust hath conceived, it bringeth forth sin: and sin, when it is finished, bringeth forth death.

Corinthians reminds us that we cannot serve both the devil and God. We choose one or the other by the conduct of our business affairs.

1 Corinthians 10:21
Ye cannot drink the cup of the Lord, and the cup of devils: ye cannot be partakers of the Lord's table, and of the table of devils.

Maintain integrity to build trust

Integrity is a word of respect used to describe leaders we trust. Their values dictate that they do the appropriate and right thing even if it is difficult or expensive. They are the rock solid leaders upon which associates feel comfortable to build their careers and stake their fortunes. However, it is not easy to maintain integrity when we live in a sinful world.

Leaders lack integrity when they entice employees or customers to trade values for inclusion into their "inner circle." These leaders are like shifting sands that do not provide a safe base on which to build a long career. Matthew warns us the path is difficult and that there are leaders who would lead us astray by promising great things with little risk. As Matthew concludes, if it sounds too good to be true it probably is; you cannot gather grapes from thorns.

> **Matthew 7:13-16**
> Enter ye in at the strait gate: for wide is the gate, and broad is the way, that leadeth to destruction, and many there be which go in there at: Because strait is the gate, and narrow is the way, which leadeth unto life, and few there be that find it. Beware of false prophets, which come to you in sheep's clothing, but inwardly they are ravening wolves. Ye shall know them by their fruits. Do men gather grapes of thorns, or figs of thistles?

James tells us that integrity requires communication with honest words and without ambiguity; a yes should be yes and a no should be no. Employees and family members may have difficulty with a direct answer but they will respect you for it. They do not respect, and they dismiss as weak, leaders whose answers straddle the line between yes and no and leave them in limbo.

> **James 5:12**
> But above all things, my brethren, swear not, neither by heaven, neither by the earth, neither by any other oath: but let your yea be yea; and your nay, nay; lest ye fall into condemnation.

Have a code of conduct

One strategic pillar that supports the business plan and vision is ethics. This pillar contains the rules of business conduct. These rules emphasize long-term thinking over the short-term manipulation of numbers to achieve this year's goals and bonuses. The ethics pillar ensures conformance with the leader's philosophies on business and governmental laws. It ensures fair treatment of employees that meet all legal requirements. Many multi-national organizations develop one set of standard ethic guidelines that meet or exceed all the regulations and laws in all the countries where they do business. A common set of standards helps to keep communications simple and streamlined across the business. It is not a simple task to get right. Saying for instance, that employees cannot accept gifts from customers may not work in some cultures where gift giving is an integral part of making acquaintances. A cultural impact review of any codes of conduct by business region is time well spent. Leaders build long-term customer relationships with trust, which they reinforce with a code of ethics. Mark reminds us with Jesus's words that leadership has a responsibility to comply with governmental laws and with God's laws.

> **Mark 12:17**
> And Jesus answering said unto them, Render to Caesar the things that are Caesar's, and to God the things that are God's. And they marveled at him.

Communicate and enforce ethical standards

Ethical standards are only wallpaper unless leadership communicates them throughout the organization in verbal and written form, and most importantly, by example. Translate the standards into local languages and post them in all locations worldwide. This shows sincerity and acts as a constant reminder of expectations. Many companies have hot line phone numbers that employees and customers can use to report an ethics violation without fear of retaliation. Outline in the communications the disciplinary action that will result from violations and enforce it. Micah tells us that God wants us to do what is right with humility and to stay on His path.

> **Micah 6:8**
> He hath shewed thee, O man, what is good; and what doth the Lord require of thee, but to do justly, and to love mercy, and to walk humbly with thy God?

Charity

A young boy asks his dad for two dollars to give to a poor man so he can buy a hot dog. The father is impressed with his son's charity and gives him the money. The son is back a few moments later and asks for another two dollars for the poor man. The dad questions why. Well says the boy, he wants to buy me a hot dog too. Charity can be contagious.

Charity is a priority

Leaders have a responsibility to reach out to all who need help, just as they reach out to help associates in their direct care. Corinthians tells us of the importance of charity and Proverbs warns us not to forget charity.

> **1 Corinthians 13:2**
> And though I have the gift of prophecy, and understand all mysteries, and all knowledge; and though I have all faith, so that I could remove mountains, and have not charity, I am nothing.
>
> **Proverbs 28:27**
> He that giveth unto the poor shall not lack: but he that hideth his eyes shall have many a curse.

There may be a temptation to put off charitable contributions until the business is financially strong. This is an error. Goals may be set so high they are not achievable, and greed may forestall charitable donations. Charity is part of God's plan and needs to be an intrinsic part of the vision for the business. The vision should address the products and services offered and how the business will interact with society. Charity is part of that interaction. If money is tight, donate time. God warns us not to store up riches for ourselves. We do not know when He will call us to judge our charitable works.

> **Luke 12:17-21**
> And he thought within himself, saying, What shall I do, because I have no room where to bestow my fruits? And he said, This will I

do: I will pull down my barns, and build greater; and there will I bestow all my fruits and my goods. And I will say to my soul, Soul, thou hast much goods laid up for many years; take thine ease, eat, drink, and be merry. But God said unto him, Thou fool, this night thy soul shall be required of thee: then whose shall those things be, which thou hast provided? So is he that layeth up treasure for himself, and is not rich toward God.

God helps people who help others

In Deuteronomy, we hear of the importance of charity and that God blesses and helps all who are charitable.

Dueteronomy14:28

At the end of three years thou shalt bring forth all the tithe of thine increase the same year, and shalt lay it up within thy gates: And the Levite, (because he hath no part nor inheritance with thee,) and the stranger, and the fatherless, and the widow, which are within thy gates, shall come, and shall eat and be satisfied; that the Lord thy God may bless thee in all the work of thine hand which thou doest.

Many organizations set up charitable trust funds to distribute profits to the needy. Businesses encourage employees to be charitable when they match employee contributions. God places a priority on charity since it shows love for our neighbor. Nehemiah tells us that we serve charity best when we share the first fruits of our labors and not only the surplus excess.

Nehemiah 10:35

And to bring the first fruits of our ground, and the first fruits of all fruit of all trees, year by year, unto the house of the Lord:

In Leviticus, we hear that we should avoid greed and always keep in our minds the need to provide for others in need.

Leviticus 19:10
And thou shalt not glean thy vineyard, neither shalt thou gather every grape of thy vineyard; thou shalt leave them for the poor and stranger: I am the Lord your God.

Extend help to the disadvantaged

Charity extends beyond giving to the poor. It also embraces the respect and assistance we give the less fortunate who need help because of handicaps, both physical and mental. In Leviticus God tells us to respect and help the handicapped. Businesses do this by charitable donations to agencies that train the handicapped to do productive work. A better way is for organizations to find employment for disadvantaged people. This makes disadvantaged people feel that they are not out-casts but useful members of society. We must respect every individual and keep the door open to help everyone who comes to us for help.

Leviticus 19:14
Thou shalt not curse the deaf, nor put a stumbling block before the blind, but shalt fear thy God: I am the Lord.

Matthew gives us God's stern warning that He will not reward people who do not recognize God's presence in people who need help.

Matthew 25:41-46
Then shall he say also unto them on the left hand, Depart from me, ye cursed, into everlasting fire, prepared for the devil and his angels: For I was an hungered, and ye gave me no meat: I was thirsty, and ye gave me no drink: I was a stranger, and ye took me not in: naked, and ye clothed me not: sick, and in prison, and ye visited me not. Then shall they also answer him, saying, Lord, when saw we thee an hungered, or athirst, or a stranger, or naked, or sick, or in prison, and did not minister unto thee? Then shall he answer them, saying, Verily I say unto you, Inasmuch as ye did it not to one of the least of these, ye did it not to me. And these

shall go away into everlasting punishment: but the righteous into life eternal.

God expects us to share the fruits of the earth, but He does not expect people who give to impoverish themselves. Corinthians tells us to work toward equality.

2 Corinthians 8:13-14
For I mean not that other men be eased, and ye burdened: But by equality, that now at this time your abundance may be a supply for their want, that their abundance also may be a supply for your want: that there may be equality:

Charity aligns us with God's plan

For an organization to be successful, it must have a strategy that is in alignment with God's benevolent and caring love for His people. In John's gospel, Jesus tells Peter that if he loves Him he should take care of others. The fact that Jesus repeats this three times shows the importance He places in this demonstration of love. Not only does Jesus want us to say we love Him but He wants us to demonstrate it by charitable acts towards others.

John 21:15-17
So when they had dined, Jesus saith to Simon Peter, Simon, son of Jonas, lovest thou me more than these? He saith unto him, Yea, Lord; thou knowest that I love thee. He saith unto him, Feed my lambs. He saith to him again the second time, Simon, son of Jonas, lovest thou me? He saith unto him, Yea, Lord; thou knowest that I love thee. He saith unto him, Feed my sheep. He saith unto him the third time, Simon, son of Jonas, lovest thou me? Peter was grieved because he said unto him the third time, Lovest thou me? And he said unto him, Lord, thou knowest all things; thou knowest that I love thee. Jesus saith unto him, Feed my sheep.

God invites leaders to do His work on earth. Leaders receive many gifts and hence God expects more from them. Luke emphasizes this point.

Luke 12:48
But he that knew not, and did commit things worthy of stripes, shall be beaten with few stripes. For unto whomsoever much is given, of him shall be much required: and to whom men have committed much, of him they will ask the more.

Leaders help others when they provide good jobs and working conditions that nurture employees and provide the means to support their families. This allows employees in turn to provide a nurturing environment that helps the family members develop their physical and moral lives. Leaders at work or at home who do these things demonstrate to God that they are doing His work on earth. God considers all of us His children. What father doing a kind act for one of his children would not please God?

Charity also extends to the treatment of the environment. We must efficiently use and handle raw materials and minimize waste products. Organizations must accept the responsibility to use efficiently the resources they take from the earth whether it is power, water, wood, air, or any other items derived from the earth's resources that God gave us. Minimize waste products and reuse as much as possible. Leaders who minimize waste do a charitable act for the environment. It is also good business. Waste is expensive. It results from the inefficient use of expensive natural resources we purchased. Its disposal is expensive. Less waste means more income for the business. Jesus gave us His perspective on waste when He fed the multitude with a few loaves and fishes. When the five thousand who had reclined to eat had been satisfied He gave instructions to His disciples to gather the surplus food and not to waste anything.

John 6:11-13
And Jesus took the loaves; and when he had given thanks, he distributed to the disciples, and the disciples to them that were

set down; and likewise of the fishes as much as they would. When they were filled, he said unto his disciples, Gather up the fragments that remain, that nothing be lost. Therefore they gathered them together, and filled twelve baskets with the fragments of the five barley loaves, which remained over and above unto them that had eaten.

Our goal at retirement

We work hard in life to help people. We hope when we retire that we can reflect back on the good works and leadership we provided for others and recite with pride the words of Timothy.

2 Timothy 4:7-8

I have fought a good fight, I have finished my course, I have kept the faith: Henceforth there is laid up for me a crown of righteousness, which the Lord, the righteous judge, shall give me at that day: and not to me only, but unto all them also that love his appearing.

Conclusion

Leadership is a challenge because of the number of things leaders need to understand and apply to govern an organization. There are many targets to hit. It may seem impossible to achieve all the things necessary to be successful. Leaders make mistakes that can devastate their confidence. When this happens, they must rely on God's love and support, calmly reassess the situation, and recover. Love is the answer. If you love your work and the people whose lives you influence, and practice this love daily, success will follow.

Romans and Corinthians summarize succinctly the qualities a manager's character must match to be a successful leader of people. It revolves around love of the work and love of the people.

Romans 13:10
Love worketh no ill to his neighbour: therefore love is the fulfilling of the law.

1 Corinthians 13:4-7
Charity suffereth long, and is kind; charity envieth not; charity vaunteth not itself, is not puffed up, Doth not behave itself unseemly, seeketh not her own, is not easily provoked, thinketh no evil; Rejoiceth not in iniquity, but rejoiceth in the truth; Beareth all things, believeth all things, hopeth all things, endureth all things.